SEEING IS BELIEVING

Books

Managing Editor *Robert Sullivan*
Director of Photography *Barbara Baker Burrows*
Deputy Picture Editor *Christina Lieberman*
Copy Editors *Barbara Gogan, Parlan McGaw*
Photo Associate *Sarah Cates*
Consulting Picture Editors
Mimi Murphy (Rome), Tala Skari (Paris)

EDITORIAL OPERATIONS
*Richard K. Prue (Director), Brian Fellows (Manager),
Richard Shaffer (Production), Keith Aurelio,
Charlotte Coco, Tracey Eure, Kevin Hart, Mert Kerimoglu,
Rosalie Khan, Patricia Koh, Marco Lau, Brian Mai,
Po Fung Ng, Rudi Papiri, Robert Pizzaro, Barry Pribula,
Clara Renauro, Katy Saunders, Hia Tan, Vaune Trachtman*

TIME HOME ENTERTAINMENT

Publisher *Jim Childs*
Vice President and Associate Publisher *Margot Schupf*
Vice President, Finance *Vandana Patel*
Executive Director, Marketing Services *Carol Pittard*
Executive Director, Business Development *Suzanne Albert*
Executive Director, Marketing *Susan Hettleman*
Publishing Director *Megan Pearlman*
Associate Director of Publicity *Courtney Greenhalgh*
Assistant General Counsel *Simone Procas*
Assistant Director, Special Sales *Ilene Schreider*
Senior Marketing Manager, Sales Marketing *Danielle Costa*
Senior Book Production Manager *Susan Chodakiewicz*
Senior Manager, Category Marketing *Bryan Christian*
Marketing Manager *Isata Yansaneh*
Associate Prepress Manager *Alex Voznesenskiy*
Associate Project Manager *Stephanie Braga*

Editorial Director *Stephen Koepp*
Senior Editor *Roe D'Angelo*
Copy Chief *Rina Bander*
Design Manager *Anne-Michelle Gallero*
Editorial Operations *Gina Scauzillo*

Special thanks: Katherine Barnet, Brad Beatson, Jeremy Biloon,
Rose Cirrincione, Assu Etsubneh, Mariana Evans, Christine Font,
Hillary Hirsch, David Kahn, Jean Kennedy, Amy Mangus, Kimberly
Marshall, Courtney Mifsud, Nina Mistry, Dave Rozzelle, Matthew
Ryan, Ricardo Santiago, Divyam Shrivastava, Adriana Tierno

Copyright © 2014 Time Home Entertainment Inc.

Published by LIFE BOOKS, an imprint of
Time Home Entertainment Inc.
1271 Avenue of the Americas, 6th floor
New York, New York 10020

ISBN 10: 1-60320-142-4
ISBN 13: 978-1-60320-142-1
Library of Congress Control Number: 2014941609

Produced in association with
KENSINGTON MEDIA GROUP
Editorial Director *Morin Bishop*
Designer *Barbara Chilenskas*
Copy Editor *Nancee Adams-Taylor*
Fact Checker *Ward Calhoun*

"LIFE" is a registered trademark of Time Inc.

We welcome your comments and suggestions
about LIFE Books. Please write to:
LIFE Books
Attention: Book Editors
PO Box 11016
Des Moines, IA 50336-1016

If you would like to order any of our hardcover Collector's Edition
books, please call us at 800-327-6388 (Monday through Friday,
7 a.m.–8 p.m., or Saturday, 7 a.m.–6 p.m. Central Time).

Page 1: Olmec Head, Mexico
De Agostini Picture Library|Getty
Pages 2-3: Crack of Silfra, Iceland
Stocktrek Images, Inc.|Alamy

These pages:
Son Doong Cave
Carsten Peter|National Geographic|Getty

SEEING IS BELIEVING

Tree-climbing goats in Morocco. Had you not seen this, would you have believed it?

INTRODUCTION
IF YOU CAN BELIEVE YOUR EYES

▶ Seeing is believing. Let's start by acknowledging that our title may be just a tiny bit misleading. Yes, there are indeed any number of topics in this book for which the visual really is the most eye-opening component. Take a gander, for example, at Son Doong Cave in Vietnam, the world's largest, and ask yourself whether words alone could ever have conveyed the immensity of this astonishing underground space that includes entire rivers and forests within its confines. Or consider the wacky saiga antelope, with its cartoonish proboscis. If you had not seen this strange creature, would you have believed it? Or sneak a peek at the otherworldly ice cave inside Langjokull Glacier in Iceland, or the elegant catacombs beneath the hard, unyielding earth of Fresno, California, built single-handedly by unschooled Sicilian immigrant Baldassare Forestiere. Had you not seen either of these exotic locations, would you have really believed they existed? And could a simple description ever have done justice to the sheer spine-tingling oddity of the Kabayan mummy caves in the Philippines, where amazingly well preserved corpses, carefully shaped into oval coffins, have been slowly deteriorating for more than 500 years? In all these cases, seeing is indeed believing.

And, of course, given that this is a LIFE book, you can be assured that the photography is compelling and topnotch and that every page offers you an opportunity to *ooh* and *ah* at an eye-catching, and frequently breathtaking, visual. In this way too, the seeing is a very large part of the believing.

But we must nonetheless admit that there are few items in our book for which the subject matter itself, quite apart from the striking images, is the genuine source of astonishment. The pictures taken on the Island of the Dolls in Mexico, for example, are certainly creepy, maybe even a bit disturbing, but it is not until one learns that the dolls were put there over the course of some 50 years by an eccentric hermit obsessed with the drowning of a young girl in the 1950s that the entire subject moves from creepy to nigh on incredible. The same can be said of the Winchester Mystery House in California: The rambling house is a little weird, with its odd stairways to nowhere, but the fact that it was built via one continuous construction project that extended over 38 years and was endlessly revised by the owner's nightly consultations with the spirit world makes the whole enterprise almost, well, unbelievable. And while the pictures of Julia Pastrana, the so-called bear-woman, are shocking, what is really unbelievable is the callous cruelty of the man who married her in order to exploit her commercial value, even continuing the ill-treatment after her death by displaying her embalmed remains in his shameful traveling show. In all these instances, were you confronted with the story outlines, you probably would have shook your head, perhaps adding emphatically, "I don't believe it!" All of which suggests yet another maxim: Truth is stranger than fiction.

Finally, there are a number of subjects that may not stretch the bounds of credulity but which we still consider genuinely amazing and more than worthy of note. These span the ages from the mystical 11,000-year-old stones in Gobekli Tepe in Turkey, to the strange Maunsell Forts erected for air defense near the mouth of the Thames River during World War II, to the eccentric Marqués de Riscal Hotel in Spain, designed just recently by innovative architect Frank Gehry. All of these provoke awe at the sheer tenacity and creativity of the questing human spirit.

Beauty too, all by itself, can produce a moment of wonder in the beholder: The lovely verdant Tunnel of Love in the Ukraine, formed by the regular passage of a train through an otherwise untended forest, falls in this category, as does the phenomenon of bioluminescence on the shores of the Maldive Islands that turns the nighttime sea a near-fluorescent blue, not to mention the serene vistas of the Salar de Uyuni in Bolivia, the largest salt flats in the world, where the horizon in every direction stretches to infinity. None of these places are impossible to believe but they are indeed impossible to fully take in until they can be seen. In these cases, we might alter the idiom just a bit: Sometimes seeing is appreciating.

So we apologize if our title does not apply with literal accuracy to every one of our covered topics. Spend some time with us—savor the pictures, enjoy the descriptions. See, learn, believe, appreciate. We think you'll enjoy the journey.

Please read more about **THE CRACK OF SILFRA** on page 13.

WATERY WONDERS

▲The surrounding forest of paperbark and eucalyptus trees provides a green contrast to Lake Hillier's shocking pink.

JEAN-PAUL FERRERO/AUSCAPE/MINDEN

THE WORLD'S PINK LAKES

Nature sometimes presents shocking colors to the human eye that defy expectations and prompt a simple question: How did that happen?

▶ No, it isn't a lake of Pepto-Bismol, just waiting to soothe the troubled tummy of some local giant. Rather, it is one of the world's so-called "pink lakes," usually produced by warm waters and a high concentration of salt, which combine to cause the large quantity of algae in certain bodies of water to generate the red pigment beta-carotene. The expanse of pink shown above is Lake Hillier, on Middle Island, in Western Australia's Recherche Archipelago. The lake is only 273 yards wide, but the contrast between its bright-pink hue and the lush green of the surrounding countryside makes for a striking sight. In some cases, such as Lake Retba, near Senegal's Cape Verde peninsula, the salt is so plentiful—the concentrations in the lake reach 40 percent—that local villagers mine the lake for it, using long shovels to extract the precious mineral from the rose-tinged water and pile it high in their boats. To protect themselves from the irritation of the salty water, the villagers rub their skin with shea butter. As warmer waters proliferate, and as the global quantities of algae increase, more and more pink lakes are blooming, including those in Canada (British Columbia), Spain (near the city of Torrevieja), and Azerbaijan (near Baku). Dusty Rose Lake in British Columbia is the odd one in the bunch, the only one in which the pinkish hue is not even partially based on salt and algae, but rather, scientists speculate, from the minerals and sediments collected by underground glacial water and then deposited in the lake.

▼These two lakes, near the Stirling Range National Park, also in Western Australia, skew a bit more towards purple than pink, though the hues can vary throughout the year.

THE CRACK OF SILFRA

An ancient crevice that shaped the world as we know it now offers divers an underwater seascape of exceptional beauty

▲ Beneath the tranquil waters of Lake Thingvallavatn lies a diver's paradise.

▶ Up in the wilds of Iceland, in Lake Thingvallavatn some 31 miles east of Reykjavik, there is a magical place called the Crack of Silfra, where the North American and Eurasian tectonic plates first separated hundreds of millions of years ago, creating the two continents with which we're now familiar. These gigantic plates continue to separate, moving .8 inches farther apart every year, causing the landmasses on the surface to shift and shake, and generating earthquakes every 10 years or so, which help to shape the undersea landscape into the distinctive series of caves and caverns that make this area a diver's paradise. The lake is fed by a glacier that used to flow directly into it but has been blocked for thousands of years by masses of volcanic lava. Today it takes the melting glacier water some 50 to 100 years to trickle underground through porous lava rock and make its way to the lake. This produces water of pristine purity, completely drinkable, and stunningly clear, providing visibility of up to 1,000 feet for the intrepid divers who venture into the exceptionally cold waters (36° to 39° Fahrenheit year round) of the crack. Though the depths near the shore are not particularly great, parts of the fissure are as deep as 207 feet; only professional divers attempt to explore there. (Amateurs tend to dive at a depth of around 23 to 40 feet.) The fissure is divided into four sections: Silfra Big Crack,

Silfra Hall, Silfra Cathedral and Silfra Lagoon. Silfra Cathedral is surely among the most breathtaking vistas on the planet, a 110-yard-long fissure with visibility up and down its entire length. The exceptional hues inside the crevice derive from the bright-green "troll hair" that, along with a variety of algae, lends the space its unusual blue-green color scheme. Those who have entered this astonishing clime come away awestruck, describing the experience as imparting a feeling of weightlessness or flying; some divers even call it "as close to a space walk as one can get without being in space."

◀ Long before the advent of the human race, the massive tectonic plates began moving apart and they continue to do so today.

THEO MOYE/ALAMY

DEEP-SEA CREATURES

At last we're getting a glimpse of these strange, sometimes terrifying, denizens of the very, very deep

▶ Ever since the first human beings gazed into the vast immensity of the sea, we have been fascinated, mesmerized and terrified—frequently all at once—by thoughts of what unimaginably exotic creatures might reside in the ocean depths. From Moby Dick to mermaids, sea monsters to selkies, gigantic octopus-like krakens to many-headed Hydras, the popular imagination has spewed forth an array of creatures over the centuries, some based on reality, some purely imagined, to feed the public fascination with the mysteries of the deep. But here's the astonishing thing: As our ability to explore those depths has increased—dramatically so in recent decades—we have discovered that the creatures that actually reside in those sometimes shockingly dark reaches of the sea are in fact more bizarre and outrageous than anything our imaginations could possibly have conjured. Herewith, we present demonstrable proof of this assertion.

◀ This 18-foot giant oarfish was found off the coast of Santa Catalina Island in Southern California.

1 Oarfish If there is a fish in existence that might have inspired the many tales of sea serpents through the years, it would unquestionably be the giant oarfish, a creature that can reach up to 600 pounds and 56 feet long, making it the longest species of bony fish. This monster has rarely been sighted through the years, preferring to remain at serious depths of around 3,300 feet, but it is certainly reasonable to speculate that a stray oarfish or two might have been seen by seafarers who returned to shore with tales of the giant fish. Recently, in October 2013, two of these enormous creatures were discovered within five days of each other on the shores of Southern California, one a mere 14 feet and the other a more respectable 18 feet (see pages 14–15). Scientists have speculated that the pair may have been driven toward the shore by powerful currents, then battered to death by exceptionally strong seas.

The oarfish is an unusual species in a number of respects. Apart from the fact that it is apparently almost inedible—too gooey and flabby—and that it eats tiny plankton and is hence essentially harmless to humans, the oarfish is the rare bony fish that lacks scales, possessing instead a skin of tubercules covered in a silvery material called guanine. (It is this silver color that has caused observers to view the oarfish as a kind of giant herring.) This unusual skin enables the oarfish to thrive under exceptionally high pressure, but makes it more susceptible to damage when the fish gets near the surface, a propensity that may have been another factor in the demise of the California duo.

Finally, we should note that among the Japanese, a particular species of oarfish (the slender oarfish) is known as the "messenger from the sea god's palace" and considered a surefire predictor of earthquakes when large quantities of the fish begin to wash ashore. Improbably enough there may be

◀ At lengths of up to 56 feet, the oarfish is the longest species of bony fish.

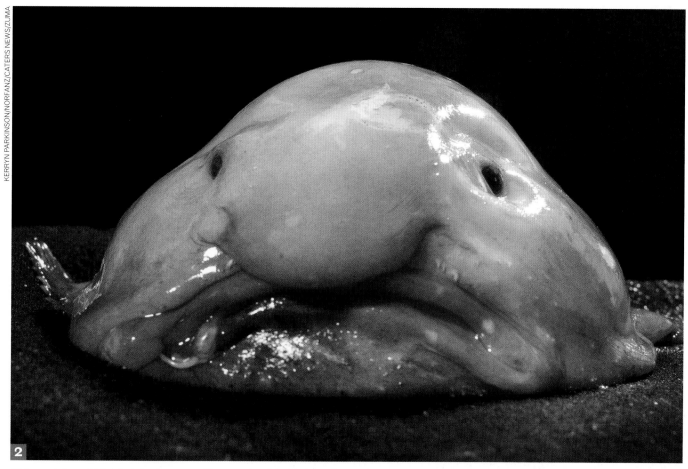

This sad-faced blobfish looks more like a normal fish when thriving in its deep-sea environment.

some truth to this ancient legend. As scientist Kiyoshi Wadatsumi told the *Japan Times*: "Deep-sea fish living near the sea bottom are more sensitive to the movements of active faults than those near the surface of the sea."

2 Blobfish What do the proboscis monkey, the pig-nosed turtle, the scrotum water frog, pubic lice and the blobfish have in common? All were nominees in a fanciful public campaign to name the world's ugliest creature from the Ugly Animal Preservation Society, a British organization dedicated to protecting many of the world's less comely but nonetheless fascinating and valuable species. "Our traditional approach to conservation is egotistical," biologist Simon Watt, the president of the society, told the BBC News. "We only protect animals that we relate to because they're cute, like pandas. If extinction threats are as bad as they seem, then focusing just on very charismatic megafauna is completely missing the point. I have nothing against pandas, but they have their supporters. These species need help."

The blobfish, with a face like Squidward from *SpongeBob SquarePants*, only squashed into a nearly horizontal shape, was the runaway winner by a plurality of some 10,000 votes, though it should be noted that the creature's blobby, gelatinous body, just slightly denser than water, is precisely what enables it to survive in the highly pressurized environment at 3,000 feet below seas level where the atmospheric pressure can be up to 120 times higher than at sea level. And in spite of its innocuous appearance, the blobfish feeds off lobsters and crabs that pass its way as it bobs along in the waters off the coast of southeastern Australia and Tasmania. Is it the ugliest creature in existence? To rephrase the popular proverb, ugliness, too, is in the eye of the beholder.

Is it any surprise that the hairy-armed Yeti crab has been compared to the abominable snowman?

3 Yeti Crab Approximately six inches long, with claws seemingly covered in fur (actually silky blond setae, very thin hairs) that do indeed resemble the arms of the legendary abominable snowman known as Yeti, this unusual species was discovered near Easter Island in the South Pacific in 2005. The Yeti crab is one of a number of species that developed on or near hydrothermal vents, which form near mid-ocean ridges—in this case the Pacific-Antarctic Ridge—where hot lava bubbles up from underneath the seafloor, producing splits in the earth's crust, heating the surrounding sea and spewing forth waters that are loaded with sulfur and metals. Highly specialized bacteria feed off this mineral stew and the Yeti crab, among others, has found ways to gain sustenance from these unusual bacteria. In a somewhat comic performance, the crabs have been observed waving their claws over the jets of warm water, thereby potentially assisting the bacteria stuck in their claw hairs to grow. Scientists need to study the matter further, but it seems possible that the Yeti crabs are thereby growing their own food on their own bodies, all at depths of 7,200 feet or more.

4 Scale Worm Of course it's unimaginably dark down near the ocean floor, so many of the species that live in these rarefied climes are blind, like the Yeti crab, or like the horrifying creature shown opposite, known as a Polychaete or scale worm, which also resides in the dense darkness near hydrothermal vents. Among other bizarre characteristics, these tiny beasts (typically an inch long,

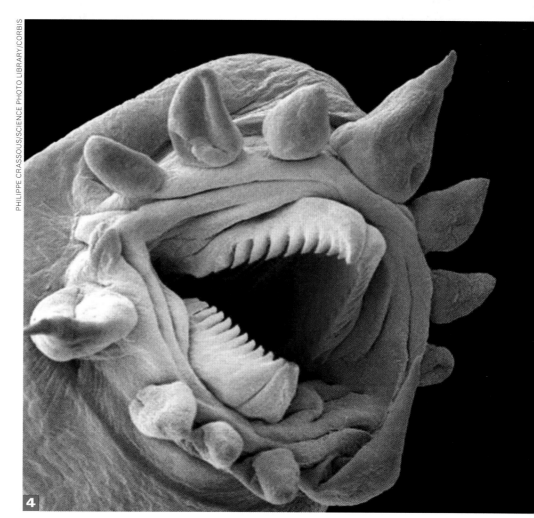

4

Be thankful this scale worm is only about an inch in length.

though there are rare examples of giant varieties that grow considerably larger) can turn their mouths inside out to reveal a fearsome set of teeth used to munch on simple organisms and bacteria that the scale worms find as they crawl along the ocean floor near a mineral-spewing vent. Yes, the blobfish is certainly unattractive, but one wonders where voters might have ranked this odd monstrosity, were it included among the nominees for ugliest creature.

5 **Dumbo Octopus** Moving from the stuff of nightmares to the land of the cute, we present another deep-sea resident, the colloquially titled Dumbo octopus, so named for the distinctive fins that protrude from its head like the ears on Disney's beloved elephant,

Dumbo. This diminutive octopus—typically only 8 to 12 inches long—has been found at depths of up to 23,000 feet, making it the deepest-dwelling octopus extant. Though rare, the Dumbo is found pretty much all over the world, testimony to its adaptability. Its mode of motion is particularly nifty: By shaking those distinctive "ears," it can hover above the ocean floor as it searches for prey; its tentacles, which spread in an umbrella shape below its mantle, enable it to scuttle quite quickly and in every direction horizontally; and that odd nose-like protuberance is actually a siphon that provides the creature with a kind of jet propulsion for additional rapid movement. All this makes the Dumbo an effective aquatic hunter, quickly moving along the ocean floor looking for the shrimp and crabs

DEEP SEA CREATURES

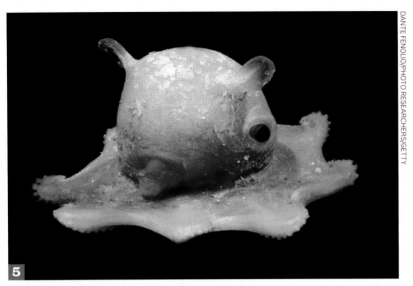

DANTE FENOLIO/PHOTO RESEARCHERS/GETTY

5

The Dumbo octopus is exceptionally agile.

NORBERT WU/SCIENCE FACTION/CORBIS

6

The barreleye is well adapted to the deep seas.

white circles in the image at left, below, are not eyes, but rather so-called "nares," large nostrils of a sort that allow the fish to find potential prey in the murky waters at 2,000 feet where these strange creatures typically hang out. That murkiness—at 2,000 feet, light is at a bare minimum, but still there in small quantities—helps explain the barreleye's distinctive eyes: large green lenses atop an unusual tubular structure, which are highly sensitive to light, capable of pointing up like highly specialized binoculars when searching for tiny jellyfish and crustaceans above, and then pointing forward when the prey is in position to be eaten, allowing the fish to actually view the food entering its own body. Talk about watching what you eat! The barreleye typically floats motionless in the deep sea as it scans the waters, then moves with remarkable accuracy to its prey, with its large pectoral fins creating exceptional stability. Just how precise can these fish be in the feeding process? One major source of sustenance for the six-inch barreleye is the siphonophores, huge jellyfish, with stinging tentacles up to 33 feet long that catch all manner of organisms, some of which the barreleye is able to extract with impunity.

7 **Giant Squid** Finally, of course, there is the giant squid, once considered a purely mythological creature, though the tales of mammoth octopus-like monsters going toe-to-toe with gigantic whales have proliferated through the years, and sailors have been reporting giant squid sightings for centuries. A number of squid carcasses seemed to confirm the animal's existence, too, but it was not until 2004 that the squid was captured in the wild in a still photograph. And it was only in 2012, in the pièce de résistance for squid research, that a team of scientists from a variety of institutions, including Japan's National Museum of Nature and Science, the Japanese broadcaster NHK

that constitute its typical diet, then dropping down on them from above before ingesting them whole. Not so dumb, this Dumbo.

6 **Barreleye Fish** The Pacific barreleye certainly possesses the criteria needed to qualify as weird, though we think this creature is, in its own way, quite beautiful, even elegant. We begin with the obvious: the barreleye has a transparent, see-through fluid-filled head. The

This stunning image is taken from the first video ever shot of a giant squid in the wild.

World and the Discovery Channel, were able to capture truly stunning video of the giant squid in all its glory in its native deep-sea environment off the coast of Japan. While much remains unknown about this elusive giant, including its specific method of hunting, we do know several things: The giant squid has enormous eyes, the largest of any animal in the world, which allow it to capture every tiny bit of light in its dark habitat; it can reach lengths of 50 to 60 feet, most of that composed of its tentacles; it is a solitary creature and never travels in groups; it can regenerate its tentacles and may deliberately sacrifice one when needed as a means of escape; and, yes, it does engage, quite frequently it seems, in battles with enormous sperm whales, this last being confirmed by the bits of giant squid frequently found in the bellies of the whales. Mythological creature, the stuff of legend and living, thriving organism—the giant squid covers all the bases.

Please read about ST. MARK'S BASILICA on page 32

MYSTICAL MARVELS

HILL OF **CROSSES**

These remarkable artifacts of faith and hope and remembrance offer vivid testimony to the tenacity of the human spirit

▲ For more than 180 years, Lithuanian believers have trekked up the Hill of Crosses.

▶ We're all familiar with the makeshift shrines to the dearly departed that sometimes spring up on the sides of highways where someone has died or on the sidewalk outside the apartment building of a beloved celebrity or on fences near the homes of the victims of inner city violence. In all of these cases, the survivors, those struggling to deal with the previously unimaginable loss of their loved ones, feel compelled to do something, anything, to express their grief. The astonishing collection of artifacts known as the Hill of Crosses in northern Lithuania began in much the same way, as the grieving families of Lithuanian rebels, killed in the struggle for freedom from the Russians, first in 1831 and again in 1863, began placing a variety of objects—first just crosses, then crucifixes, carvings, statues of the Virgin Mary, rosaries and miniature effigies—on a hill some seven miles north of Siauliai. During the era of Soviet occupation from 1944 to 1990, the hill became a symbol

▲This is just a small sampling of the more than 100,000 objects, many of them handmade, now on the hill.

of peaceful resistance and of the Lithuanians' refusal to relinquish their distinct heritage, culture and religion. The authorities threatened to destroy the site many times, including attempts to bulldoze it in 1963 and 1973. In the end, while some 6,200 objects were destroyed, the hill lived on, a tribute to faith and persistence and stubborn resistance.

Pope John Paul II traveled to the site in 1993 and a plaque commemorates his visit with these words: "Thank you, Lithuanians, for this Hill of Crosses which testifies to the nations of Europe and to the whole world the faith of the people of this land." Current estimates place the number of objects on the hill at more than 100,000.

COLOSSAL HEADS OF OLMEC

Remnants of an ancient Mesoamerican civilization, these striking sculptures suggest a creative, highly organized society

▶ It is tragic how little we know of the first great Mesoamerican civilization, the Olmecs, who thrived along the Gulf of Mexico in the current districts of Veracruz and Tabasco, from approximately 1200 to 400 B.C., and whose culture and society greatly influenced the civilizations that followed, most notably the Maya and the Aztec. But at least we have this remarkable collection of 17 stone heads, representative, it is now thought, of actual, individual rulers of this great civilization. The heads, varying in size from 5 to 11 feet high and weighing between 6 and 50 tons, are carved on the front and sides and typically flat in back. They were generally sculpted from large spherical boulders of basalt, though several were refashioned from pre-existing sculptures of massive thrones. The facial characteristics— chubby cheeks and flat noses—are still commonly found among the peoples along the Gulf of Mexico. The distinctive helmets worn by the heads led to the speculation at one point that these were depictions of Mesoamerican ballplayers, but the effort and the number

CHICO SANCHEZ/AURORA PHOTOS/CORBIS

▲ The distinctive facial features of the Olmec heads can still be found among indigenous peoples near the Gulf of Mexico.

◄ Stirling, with his wife, Marion (both with hands on statue), found the first head in San Lorenzo in 1945.

of people needed to produce these massive sculptures have persuaded scholars that only a powerful ruler could have marshaled the resources necessary to produce such works. One of these colossal heads was discovered in Tres Zapotes, Mexico, in the 19th century, but it was not until American Matthew Stirling found the first head in San Lorenzo Tenochtitlán, Mexico, in 1945—erosion had worn away the surface earth to reveal an eye—that the extent of the Olmecs' creativity became apparent. Ten heads would be uncovered in San Lorenzo. The work needed to produce these heads was prodigious. Many of the boulders had to be moved 90 miles and more, and for a civilization without wheels or beasts of burden, this was a major accomplishment indeed. Transport by water was used when possible, but causeways, ramps and roads were surely needed as well, along with a small army of human helpers who had to be housed, clothed and fed.

KARAHUNJ

These ancient stones in Armenia present more curious questions than definitive answers

▲ Karahunj at sunset: Were the stones intended to mark a grave or to direct observers to significant points in the heavens?

▶ Is this the Armenian Stonehenge? There certainly are many similarities: a larger, outer circle of stones surrounding a smaller interior circle, though the stones are considerably smaller than Stonehenge's—the largest weigh only 10 tons and are only nine feet tall; an ancient lineage, yes, though Karahunj is actually at least 2,000 years older than Stonehenge. Finally, there is some evidence that both sites were primarily used as burial grounds—there are some 200 shallow graves covered by massive stone slabs on the grounds of Karahunj, though, as with burial sites in Stonehenge, the relationship of these graves to the central circles is less than clear. Beyond these surface similarities, little is known, and speculation about the various ways in which Karahunj might have been used rages unabated. One common theory is that the location represents the oldest known astronomical observatory. In support of this idea is one odd characteristic of Karahunj, not found in Stonehenge: 84 of the stones have carefully bored holes at different angles in them, some of which seem to point to various celestial points of significance. The holes are also offered as the reason for the name of the location, with *kara* meaning "stones" and *hunj* meaning "voices," the presumption being that the wind whistling through the holes in the stones created a distinctive sound.

ST. MARK'S BASILICA

Perhaps the world's most ornate and richly adorned cathedral, St. Mark's Basilica is a golden masterpiece

▶ The stunning St. Mark's Basilica in Venice is, to a certain extent, a tribute to the cultural advantages of creative looters with an eye for fine art, since a surprisingly high percentage of the gold and marble and statuary that make the cathedral so eye-catching was added to the structure as a result of the Crusaders who came back from their plundering raids in the 12th and 13th centuries with massive quantities of booty, to be distributed wherever they saw fit. The overwhelming impression one receives when standing before this astonishingly complex yet somehow symmetrical structure is of a cathedral dipped in liquid gold on the outside and sprayed with it all over the walls of the interior. Gleaming, glittering, glinting—the gold shines forth from every angle and in the evening the gold on the exterior catches fire with the setting sun. The structure, which combines both Byzantine and Gothic elements, is almost ludicrously ornate, with statues—the most

notable being St. Mark, who stands atop the highest rooftop on the front of the building, with the winged lion that is his symbol directly below—and friezes, and mosaics and complex constellations of columns adorning virtually every available space both inside and outside the cathedral. Consecrated sometime between A.D. 1084 and 1117—two earlier structures on the site were destroyed—the building was originally the chapel of the doge, or leader, of the Republic of Venice, then one of the preeminent powers in Europe. Over the years, the basilica took on additional civic significance, with all the important ceremonial functions taking place in the chapel, including the installation of the doges, who were selected by the local elites and whose palace sits right next door. Finally, beginning in 1807, after the end of the Venetian Republic, the church came under the aegis of the Roman Catholic Church, thereby becoming in essence the official cathedral of Venice.

▲When the waters from the Venetian canals overflow into the piazza in front of the cathedral, the effect is unforgettable.

▲ Fanciful drawings, a strange indecipherable alphabet—are these the products of a hoax, perhaps perpetrated by Voynich himself (opposite), or the genuine record of a long-lost language?

THE VOYNICH MANUSCRIPT

A strange little book has prompted a spate of feverish investigation—and a wealth of controversy—since its release to the world in 1912

MARY EVANS PICTURE LIBRARY/ALAMY

▶ Now this is a tale of mystifying proportions. In 1912, a rare book dealer named Wilfrid Voynich claimed to be in possession of a puzzling manuscript, filled with a language no one could recognize, in an alphabet no one had ever seen, with botanical and astronomical drawings of earthly and heavenly objects heretofore unknown to the human family. Voynich was of the belief that the manuscript was created by philosopher and alchemist Roger Bacon (c. 1220–1292), and he had an accompanying letter from 1666 to further bolster his claim about the provenance of this odd little book—at 9 x 6 inches, the volume is barely larger than a mass-market paperback. Recent analysis of the vellum and ink used in the document supports a 15th century dating of the document, which would eliminate Bacon as the author. But what does it mean? And what does it say? In nearly a century since, a battalion of the world's experts have endeavored to translate, decode or otherwise explain the meaning of this document. Linguists have analyzed the text and the characters, with some declaring the distribution of characters to be consistent with a European language and others finding the "language" suspicious—for example, there are almost no words shorter than two letters or longer than 10. William Friedman, a key figure from the early days of the now infamous National Security Agency (NSA) and one of the world's most celebrated cryptographers, saw the document not as reflective of some lost, indecipherable language but rather as a complex sort of code to be cracked. Alas, in spite of his best efforts, he was unable to make sense of the manuscript when he studied it at length in the 1950s. Theories have proliferated ever

since. Could this be a constructed language? Or a "letter-based cipher," with the original document converted into the manuscript's strange alphabet through an algorithm of some kind? Could the meaning only be present in certain parts of the book, in certain letters, or certain pen strokes? Or is it actually possible that this is a truly lost language, written perhaps in an invented alphabet? Finally, could the entire collection of markings be nothing but nonsense?

The simple answer is that no one knows. Not surprisingly, given the suspicious nature of 21st century observers, there are many who believe the entire document to be a hoax by Wilfrid Voynich himself, who certainly would have known, and been able to acquire, the materials and inks to create a believable forgery. Presumably his motive would have been financial—such a manuscript from the pen of Roger Bacon would have been quite valuable. And any intelligent con artist would know that forging an additional document, like the letter that accompanied the book, would be a wise ploy to further support the book's authenticity. An ethnic Pole who grew up in Lithuania, Voynich ended up running a secondhand bookstore in London, frequented by Karl Marx and, among others, a man named Sidney Reilly, known as the Ace of Spies, whose suspicious but well-documented activity at the British Museum library prior to Voynich's announcement of the manuscript included the study of a book entitled *Some Observations on Ancient Inks*. The manuscript now sits in the famed Beinecke Rare Book & Manuscript Library at Yale, and a digitized high-resolution copy is free to view online. Take a look and reach your own conclusions.

◄ The elaborate carvings on the stones are as mysterious as their placement. Anthropologists will continue to speculate about their meaning, but we may never know for sure.

► Circles abound in Gobekli Tepe—frequently circles upon circles in fact—but what do they mean?

GOBEKLI TEPE

Some 6,000 years before Stonehenge, was this site in Turkey the first place of worship?

► Sometimes, in archaeology as in so many other areas of study, one has to look carefully to avoid reaching hasty conclusions. That is certainly one lesson to be gleaned from the case of Gobekli Tepe in Turkey, one of the most astonishing and potentially significant archaeological sites in the world. Back in the 1960s, a team of anthropologists from Istanbul University and the University of Chicago made a survey of the area and dismissed the slabs of limestone as merely evidence of an abandoned medieval cemetery. It was not until a German archaeologist named Klaus Schmidt returned to the site in 1994 and made a much more extensive examination that the world learned what was really there: huge stones, many of them covered with carvings of dangerous creatures like lions and vultures and scorpions and spiders and snakes, all dating back some 11,000 years, fully 6,000 years before Stonehenge. And what Schmidt discovered when his team began to excavate the area more fully was even more astonishing: Beneath the initial layer of soil on the hilltop location—Gobekli Tepe means "belly hill"

in Turkish—Schmidt found giant megaliths in the shape of the letter *T*, surrounded by 7- to 10-ton stone pillars, some as tall as 16 feet, arranged in circles of up to 65 feet in diameter. As the digging went deeper, the scientists were amazed to find that beneath the first circle of stone was another similar one, and beneath that yet another, with the entire 50-foot height of the hill composed of one buried ring on top of another. (The team also excavated similar rings nearby.)

Just as interesting as the many fascinating discoveries made by the German team were the things they did *not* find, most notably any of the signs of habitation one might expect to find in an area where people actually lived, i.e., cooking hearths, houses, trash pits or any of the clay figurines that were typically found in contemporaneous residential sites in the area. Keep in mind that the people of this very ancient period were hunter-gatherers, agriculture was still unknown and writing was still 6,000 years in the future. Given all these facts, Schmidt is firmly convinced that Gobekli Tepe

represents the oldest known example of a temple, or place of worship, in the world. And if he is right about that, his discovery turns on its head one of the most accepted views about how civilization began among the human race. The conventional wisdom holds that it was not until the development of agriculture and the communities that naturally accompanied an agrarian lifestyle that humans were able to develop the skills and marshal the time and energy necessary to build temples and other examples of sophisticated society. The example of Gobekli Tepe, however, suggests precisely the reverse—namely, that the development of the monoliths and other stone constructions predated agriculture and may in fact have laid the groundwork for the communities and social structures that followed. Given the coordinated effort required to build the many rings and carve the many stones of Gobekli Tepe—Schmidt points out that this would have required hundreds of workers, all of whom would have to be housed and fed and supported in communities of some kind—the premise has now

been reversed: As noted by Stanford archaeologist Ian Hodder, "This shows sociocultural changes come first, agriculture comes later. You can make a good case this area is the real origin of complex Neolithic societies."

And just what were the religious beliefs of this early society? And what purpose might these circles and carvings have served? The images carved into the stone pillars at Gobekli Tepe were not those of gazelles or boars or sheep or deer, the animals that constituted the bulk of the human diet at the time, but rather the creatures of nightmares, the lions and scorpions that bit or stung, and the vultures that carried carrion away and were seemingly even then a symbol of the death that awaited everyone. Might this site have been a place to seek protection against such dangers from some notion of a deity? Or was the hill in fact a burial ground where the dead could lie amidst the society's symbols of the gods and the afterlife and gaze out on the valley below? No one knows the answers to these questions just yet, but the search continues.

CHRIST OF THE ABYSS

The figure of Christ, found throughout the world, has a striking presence beneath the sea as well

▶ While scuba diving is now viewed as an almost entirely safe and fun way to explore and enjoy the worlds beneath the sea, it has not always been so. One of the earliest diving pioneers—in fact the first Italian to use scuba gear—was a man named Dario Gonzatti, who tragically died in the waters off San Fruttuoso on the Italian Riviera. In his honor, fellow diver Duilio Marcante came up with the idea of a statue of Christ to be placed in the water near where Gonzatti died. Sculptor Guido Galletti created the piece, melting medals, naval artifacts and bells in order to get the quantity of bronze he needed, and the figure was placed underwater, on the floor of the sea 50 feet below, in 1954. A bit over eight feet tall, the figure depicts Christ with hands and face upraised, seemingly beseeching God for his benediction on the tragedy that took place there. Every July, on the beach in San Fruttuoso, a torchlight mass is conducted to honor all those who lost their lives at sea.

Two more statues were created from the same mold. The first was donated to the people of Grenada for their help in rescuing passengers and crew from the Italian ship *Bianca C*, which caught fire and sank near the harbor of St. George's in 1961. Through the help and quick action of the local authorities, all but one of the 673 people aboard the ship were saved. The statue now stands on a wall at the edge of the harbor. Finally, a third version was created and placed off the coast of Florida, near Key Largo, in 1965. With an enormous anchoring pedestal, the statue has survived stormy seas of all sorts, including several hurricanes, and remains in place, submerged in only 25 feet of water, where interested tourists can even view the figure from the surface of the sea.

◀ This figure, off the coast of Key Largo, Florida, has been offering underwater blessings since 1965.

GOLDEN ROCK OF BURMA

For centuries, Buddhist believers have been making the pilgrimage to this holy—and astounding—site in southern Myanmar

STEVE MCCURRY/MAGNUM

▲The golden rock takes on an even more glittery aspect when struck by the rays of the setting sun.

▶ From November through March they come, just as they have for centuries, thousands of Buddhist pilgrims, to trek up Mt. Kyaiktiyo to this sacred place in southern Myanmar, mesmerized by the golden rock that seems ready to tumble from its precarious perch at any moment, and the elegant pagoda that sits serenely on top, seemingly unconcerned about its perilous position. Legend has it that the rock, 25 feet high and 50 feet in circumference, is held in place by a single strand of hair from the Buddha, but one need not accept such a mythical construction to be awed by a sense of wonder when beholding this holy site. Today, one can take a bus to within about a mile of the rock and,

shedding one's shoes as required by Buddhist custom, make the final climb barefoot; but the most devoted, or at least the most physically fit, make the longer trek of approximately seven miles from the village of Kinpun. Near the pagoda, throughout the night, believers chant, light candles and offer prayers to the Buddha. The men—and only the men—are allowed to actually touch the rock and add their own gold leaves to the thousands already plastered on the surface, and thereby help to maintain the distinctive golden hue of the holy stone. This fervor reaches a climax during the Full Moon Day of Tabaung in March, when the pagoda is illuminated by 90,000 candles.

◄ Prayers are offered day and night by pilgrims who gather at the foot of one of Buddhism's most revered shrines.

▲ The passageways inside the tumuli are adorned with yet more hand-carved stones.

CARNAC STONES

There is no larger collection of prehistoric stones in the world than this stunning assemblage in the French countryside

▶ Some 5,000 years after the monoliths of Gobekli Tepe were erected, the stones of Carnac, approximately 3,000 of them—the largest such collection of prehistoric stones in the world—were being placed in the countryside of Brittany, mostly inside the borders of what is now Carnac. The stones fall into four categories: Some are arranged in alignments (long rows of standing stones from 2 to 13 feet high stretching up to 4,300 feet); others in dolmens (little hut-like structures with a collection of stones supporting a capstone or roof); still others under mounds of earth called tumuli, creating a kind of tomb, with a central passageway leading to an inner central vault where artifacts associated with the deceased were stored; and finally some as single stand-alone menhirs, many as tall as almost 20 feet. What does it all mean? As with all these prehistoric sites, the answer is not clear and multiple answers have been advanced.

▲ Many experts believe that each stone in the long lines of stones represents a clan leader.

One posits that the stones are aligned for astronomical observation, another that the stones sit in a seismically highly active area and as such were intended to be detectors for potential earthquakes. In the end, given the clear funereal purpose associated with the dolmens and the tumuli, the most likely theory seems to be that the entire area was a large burial ground, with each piece in the extended rows of stones perhaps representing the leader of one of the several chiefdoms some historians believe dominated the area in this period. (Are the crosses in Arlington National Cemetery so different?) Under this theory, the largest stones would be the earliest, most revered leaders, the George Washingtons of the age if you will, and the smaller stones indicative of the later leaders whose dwindling authority signaled the end of this era.

DEAD AND GONE

Please read about the MORTUARY TEMPLE OF HATSHEPSUT on page 48.

KABAYAN MUMMY CAVES

Deep in the Filipino forests, these mummies have kept their spooky vigil for hundreds of years

► One can only imagine what terror must have been struck in the hearts of the workers who first discovered ancient burial caves when they began logging activity in the forests of the Benguet district north of Manila in the early 20th century. There they were, minding their own business, when they were suddenly confronted with scores of mummies and skulls placed in coffins, untouched for centuries, many of them eerily well preserved. In fact, these are the remains of what most experts believe were the leaders of the Ibaloi tribe, placed in the caves between A.D. 1200 and 1500 and preserved through one of the world's most elaborate mummification processes: First the dying person imbibes a very salty drink intended to begin the process of drying the body's internal fluids. Then, after death, the body is placed in a chair over a fire with just enough heat to further dry the bodily fluids without burning the body itself. Next, tobacco smoke is blown down the body's throat to dry the internal organs. Finally, herbs are rubbed on the body to help preserve it. This process might take weeks or perhaps even months, before the body, shaped into a fetal position, is finally placed in an oval, wooden coffin, typically covered in decorative carvings. Sadly, ever since the discovery of the burial caves, looters have been at work, stealing some of the mummies and otherwise desecrating the site, a practice that continues to this day to some extent in spite of the limited protections put in place by the National Museum of the Philippines and the World Monuments Fund.

▲ Carefully shaped into their oval coffins in a variety of poses, some of these mummies seem almost alive.

ALEXIS DUCLOS/GAMMA

▲ The many-tiered temple would not be out of place among the classical buildings of Greece.

MORTUARY TEMPLE
OF HATSHEPSUT

Egypt's first female pharaoh commissioned one of her country's most memorable structures

► In the annals of groundbreaking women, there should be a special niche reserved for Hatshepsut, the first female pharaoh of Egypt and, some believe, the first queen in history, period. Given the lack of historical precedent, her decision to assume the throne after the death of her husband, Pharaoh Tuthmose II, and before she was able to bear a son, was clearly an act of exceptional courage, not to mention ambition. She went on to rule long and effectively, from 1479 to 1458 B.C., establishing a reputation as one of Egypt's most prolific builders and the pharaoh responsible for rebuilding Egypt's sadly diminished trade networks. Among her greatest creations was her own elegant mortuary temple, seemingly cut from the severe cliffs that rise behind it and considered by many to be Egypt's closest approximation to what in the West would be called classical architecture. Her chancellor, the royal architect Senenmut, was in charge of the project. A 100-foot causeway leads to the temple, which is distinguished by three layered terraces running the length of the temple that climb to a height of 97 feet. Inside, the temple walls and its many chambers are covered in stunning pictorial reliefs, many of them depicting the story of Hatshepsut herself as well as the tale of an expedition to the exotic Land of Punt on the Red Sea. The temple is notable for enabling, indeed even encouraging, active worship within its walls, a significant departure from previous designs.

CITY OF THE DEAD

For many Egyptians, Cairo's massive necropolis offers better living conditions than they can find in the city proper

▲ Children play in the City of the Dead, apparently unaware that they are doing so inside a mausoleum.

▶ It is a fine line, indeed, that separates the living from the dead. No one who follows world and local events in even the most cursory way can fail to recognize this existential reality. Floods and famine and earthquakes, not to mention terrorist attacks, mass murders and ethnic violence, all serve to reinforce how fleeting life can be and how surrounded we are by the inevitability of death. But there may be no place on earth where the thin and permeable tissue that divides life from death is more apparent than in the vast four-mile-long necropolis in Cairo, known as el-Arafa, or the City of the Dead, a web of tombs and

mausoleums founded in the 7th century A.D. Some two million bodies are housed here, along with approximately 500,000 living and breathing human beings, who have taken up residence inside the buildings and chambers, some of them quite ornate, which were originally built as homes for only the dead. Some of these families have been living in the City of the Dead for generations, with the original occupant being a caretaker of the graves and mausoleum for a wealthy family, but the numbers in this unusual neighborhood have grown exponentially as a chronic housing shortage in Cairo, along with a wave of

▲ The clothes of the living hang on the doors of the dead in this most unusual neighborhood.

migration from impoverished rural areas, has produced more people than the sprawling city can accommodate. For many, the opportunities in the necropolis—most of the tombs are housed in a simple structure that can easily be converted into a home with a lock on the door—are far better than in the teeming Cairene slums. Some of the families of longer standing have gardens, a villa with walls, and roofs over their heads, a style of life generally associated with more affluent Egyptians. And while services are limited—though many have electricity and running water, some do not—and while the residents for the most part have no legal right to live where they do, a thriving and vibrant community has emerged and it is generally viewed as highly unlikely that any future Egyptian government will want to take on the daunting disruptions that would be produced by any effort to evict the residents. And so they live on, picking up odd jobs, trading goods among themselves, or earning small fees for caring for the graves of wealthy Egyptians. "Life here is peaceful," one elderly resident told *National Geographic*. "Living with the dead is a good thing for an old person. They don't talk, and they are very still."

CAPUCHIN CATACOMBS OF PALERMO

Filled with more than 8,000 bodies, this gruesome display of death is among Sicily's most popular tourist attractions

▶ In spite of the popularity of horror movies often featuring gruesome modes of demise, Americans are not comfortable with the subject of death. When confronted with the real thing, without the distancing effects of over-the-top computer-generated imagery or the standard conventions of the horror genre, we tend to turn away. Violence and killing grab our attention; death itself, not so much. Nonetheless, it is hard not to engage in a kind of sickly fascination when confronted with the catacombs of the Capuchin monks, on the outskirts of the Sicilian city of Palermo, where 8,000 bodies, many of them mummified, are arrayed, posed or otherwise presented in various states of decomposition, for the delectation of the viewing public. Brother Silvestro of Gubbio was the first man to be mummified and placed in the catacombs in

◀ These embalmed residents of the catacombs may appear to be chatting while in line at the bank, but in fact they have been dead for at least a century or two.

in 1599, when the cemetery neighboring the Capuchin monastery finally ran out of real estate. Over the next three centuries, the residents of the catacombs expanded beyond the original intention to inter only monks and came to include women and children and citizens of distinction as well, whose families paid a fee for their loved ones to be in the now-trendy catacombs. Bodies were typically dried on ceramic pipes, then washed in vinegar, and sometimes embalmed or sealed in glass cabinets. Eventually the bodies were divided into several "corridors," including separate sections for men, women, virgins, children, priests, monks and professionals. They were clothed as requested by their families or as appropriate, with priests and monks in clerical garb; in some cases, distinguished local citizens even had their clothes regularly changed. The last monk to be interred in the catacombs was Brother Riccardo in 1871; the last interment of any kind took place in the 1920s, with one of the last residents of all being Rosalia Lombardo, dead at two years old, but still stunningly well preserved through a complex embalming method that included formalin (to kill bacteria), alcohol (to dry the body), glycerine (to prevent overdrying), salicylic acid (to destroy fungi) and zinc salts (to maintain the body's rigidity). In spite of its less than cheery atmosphere, the catacombs of the Capuchins remain one of Sicily's most popular tourist attractions.

CAPUCHIN CATACOMBS OF PALERMO

YANN ARTHUS-BERTRAND/CORBIS

BETTMANN/CORBIS

▲ In some cases, the skulls of the dearly departed have become decorative elements in elaborate displays.

► Much of the catacombs are divided into distinct corridors for the various classes of people interred there, including separate sections for men, women, virgins and priests.

MAURICE BRANGER/ROGER-VIOLLET/GETTY

PORT OF MUYNAK

An ill-considered decision by Soviet planners led to the shrinking of the Aral Sea to disastrous proportions

▲ This rusting hulk, once part of a thriving fishing industry, now serves only as shelter for a herd of camels.

▶ It is hard to look at the rotting shipwrecks sitting useless in the sands of western Uzbekistan without thinking of Percy Bysshe Shelley's immortal poem about Ozymandias, the now-forgotten ruler, whose once fearsome statue lies neglected and broken in pieces in the sand of some "antique land," mocked by the words on the pedestal: "Look on my works, ye mighty, and despair!" These ships, like Ozymandias, once had pride of place, too, as part of a thriving fishing industry in the town of Muynak, on the edge of the Aral Sea, which employed 40,000 people and produced one-sixth of all the fish caught in the Soviet Union. Alas, the misguided decision in the 1940s by Soviet planners to begin diverting water from the rivers that fed the Aral in order to irrigate the desert and try to grow a variety of crops there had disastrous consequences. The level of the Aral Sea fell by an average of eight inches a year in the 1960s, 20 to 24 inches a year in the '70s, and 31 to 35 inches in the '80s. By 2007, the sea was just 10 percent of its original size and the once prosperous port of Muynak was now many miles from the nearest shore. Sadly, agricultural chemical runoff has severely polluted the remaining seabed and powerful winds produce poisonous dust storms that threaten the health of even the few residents that remain.

▲ From a distance the forts look like something out of science fiction, but a closer look (opposite) reveals the degree of decay.

MAUNSELL ARMY FORTS

At a most perilous time in British history, these forts stood as a last line of defense against Hitler's bombers

▶ In the dark days of 1942, with France under German occupation, and Hitler seriously eyeing a potential invasion of England, the British government was seeking every means at its disposal to defend itself against a German onslaught. It was in this environment that three sets of seven forts were built and placed in the waters near the mouth of the Thames Estuary. The four-legged Maunsell Forts, named after designer Guy Maunsell, may look more like something from *The Empire Strikes Back* than like a military installation, but five of the forts in each array of seven carried serious anti-aircraft artillery—a seventh was placed farther out than the others and included the spotlight that scanned the skies for German aircraft—and the Thames forts ultimately shot down 22 enemy aircraft and 30 V-1 flying bombs. Today these forts sit in splendid isolation—for the most part no longer connected by the walkways that were in place during the war—but still a vivid reminder of a perilous time when the world teetered on the brink of fascist domination. Of course, even such significant icons can be used for other purposes: Several forts were used as pirate radio stations in the 1960s.

Please read about THE CAVE OF CRYSTALS on page 64.

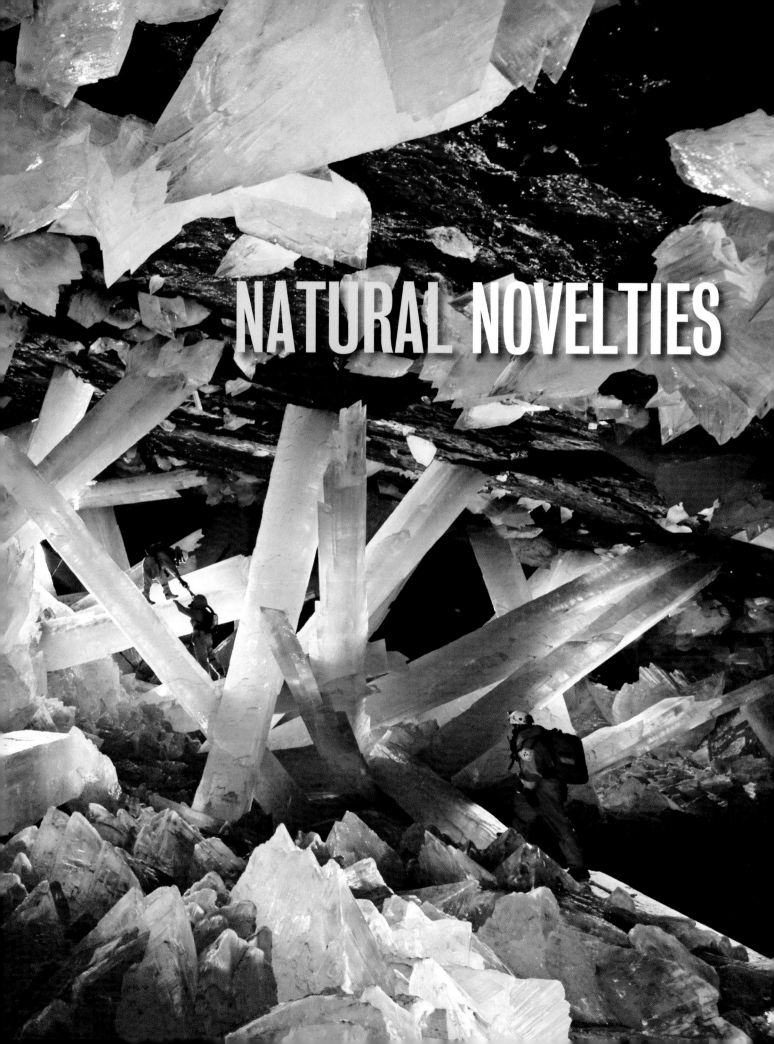

NATURAL NOVELTIES

SALAR DE UYUNI

High in the Andes, there is a landscape of dreams, where the horizon seems to stretch to infinity in every direction

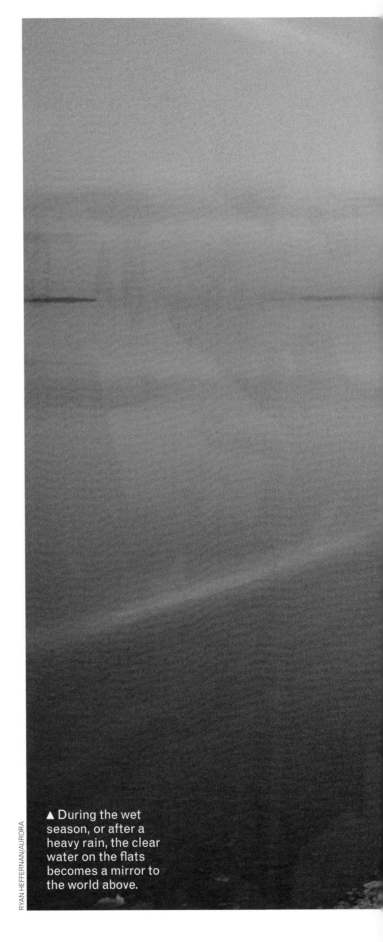

▶ This stunning landscape, set high in the Bolivian Andes at an elevation of 12,000 feet, is called Salar de Uyuni, the largest of the salt flats in the world, with a surface area of 4,086 square miles. Just how flat are the flats? The average altitude variation across the entire area of the Salar is less than a single meter. Consisting of a top layer of salt about 10 feet thick—the flats are estimated to contain 11 billion tons of salt—above an underlying pool of brine, the flats are what is left of a gigantic prehistoric lake that went dry thousands of years ago. As valuable as the salt is, the most valuable natural resource in the area may be lithium, a critical component in the batteries used in all sorts of electronic devices, though much of the lithium contained in the Salar brine has yet to be extracted and there remains some doubt about whether the Bolivian government will allow foreign companies to be involved. This is starkly beautiful terrain, with the seemingly endless horizontal plain broken only by the pyramids of salt dug from the turf and waiting to be harvested, or by the stray specimen of giant cactus—some are as tall as 39 feet—one of the only plants hardy enough to grow in the salt. During the wet season, or after a heavy rain, the entire Salar is transformed into a mammoth lake, whose crystalline waters perfectly mirror the skies above. One final oddity in this most unusual locale: On the edge of the Salar there is a hotel made entirely of salt. There is no electricity and water must be trucked to the location, but it is hard to imagine a quieter, more serene environment than this: alone on the flats, a preposterously large star-filled sky above, mirrored in the endless water-filled flats below.

▲ During the wet season, or after a heavy rain, the clear water on the flats becomes a mirror to the world above.

RYAN HEFFERNAN/AURORA

CAVE OF THE CRYSTALS

Deep underground in northern Mexico, these gigantic crystals have been forming for hundreds of thousands of years

▲ Crystals of every size and shape jut out at crazy angles from every surface.

▶ There may be no phenomenon documented in this book more worthy of the idiom "seeing is believing" than this utterly astonishing cave in northern Mexico filled with the most gigantic crystals the world has ever seen. To witness these natural marvels one must descend about 1,000 feet below the earth's surface, deeper even than the lead and silver mine that employed the pair of brothers who first broke through the floor of the Naica mine to discover this miraculous limestone cavern in 2000. Inside the cave, the crystals present themselves in crazy profusion, seemingly sprouting from every surface as they intersect one another at unlikely angles, formed into a variety of shapes and colors. The largest discovered to date has been measured at a length of 39 feet, a diameter of 13 feet and a weight of 55 tons. The age of these crystals has been estimated at 500,000 years old.

No one can stay in this environment for long: The temperature remains at least 114° Fahrenheit with 90 to 100 percent humidity, stiflingly moist and warm, presenting a constant risk of heatstroke. Those who have ventured into this underground wonderland describe the experience as almost religious, as if the awe inspired by these unimaginably

▲ The stifling heat limits the amount of time any human can remain in this magical environment.

ancient, inconceivably large and unspeakably beautiful objects somehow suggests a realm beyond our own.

An understanding of how these crystals formed only enhances this sense of awe. For while the surface world went through cataclysmic changes above them, the crystals remained at peace in their unchanging world below, taking shape in a watery bath, heated by magma in the ground farther down and loaded with calcium sulfate and minerals that convert to selenite, the basic building block of the crystals, at a constant temperature of 136° Fahrenheit. For thousands and thousands of years, the crystals thrived in this seemingly eternal stew, getting bigger and bigger, until suddenly in 1985, human agency upset the chemical applecart and the mining company's giant pumps succeeded in lowering the water table and thereby draining the cave.

THE CHELYABINSK METEOR

While the world wasn't looking, a blindingly bright meteor blazed across central Russia, wreaking havoc along the way

▲ A hole 20 feet across was unmistakable evidence of the meteorite that slammed into Lake Chebarkul.

▶ No one saw it coming. While scientists had their eyes and their telescopes trained on a large asteroid called 2012 DA14 that made a close but harmless pass over the South Atlantic, a much smaller meteor was hurtling toward Earth on an unusually shallow trajectory and approaching from the east quite close to the rising sun over central Russia, making it even harder to detect. Soon, however, the stealth meteor would be impossible to miss as it made its 18-second run across Russia, its light so blindingly bright—30 times brighter than the sun—that some observers had their skin burned by its ultraviolet rays, and the explosion from its breakup at approximately 17 miles above Earth so powerful that over 7,200 buildings were damaged and scores of people were injured by flying glass and debris resulting

▲ Russians were stunned by the sight of the meteor streaking across the morning sky.

from the blast. Scientists later estimated the meteor's size at 65 feet wide and its speed when it entered Earth's atmosphere at 42,500 miles per hour. It was the largest object from space to descend to Earth since the Tunguska meteor in 1908, which flattened several hundred miles of Siberian forest. The Chelyabinsk meteor was the first such event in the age of social media, and within hours of its descent, amateur videos were flooding the Internet, with observers reporting intense heat from a fireball streaking across the sky and a loud boom that split the air several minutes later. The meteorites that resulted from its breakup fell in a shower throughout the area, one of the largest pieces crashing into Lake Chebarkul, 43 miles southwest of Chelyabinsk, leaving a 20-foot-wide hole in its icy surface.

TUNNEL OF LOVE

Man and nature collaborated to produce this beautiful passage through the woods

▶ In western Ukraine, far from the recent troubles with Russia, there is a place in the forest called Kleven, where a three-kilometer section of railroad leads to a fiberboard factory, thereby providing the wood needed for the day's work. As it has made its route, three times a day, trip after trip, day after day, year after year, the train has carved a striking tunnel of green from the dense, otherwise untended forest, shaped to the contours of the train car itself. Now this enticing tunnel of green has become a place of legend: It is said that if a pair of lovers crosses the tunnel and sincerely makes a wish while holding hands, the magic of the tunnel and the surrounding forest will make it come true.

SINGING
THE BLUES

The phenomenon of bioluminescence produces sensational seaside light shows as the ocean is illuminated in a burst of blue

▶ A deserted beach on Vaadhoo Island in the Maldives may be the best spot in the world to observe the phenomenon of bioluminescence, which takes a normal stretch of dark ocean water near the shore at nighttime and brightly illuminates it with a striking blue light. Did someone install underwater bulbs when no one was looking? No, the light is produced by tiny phytoplankton, seafaring microbes, that emit this blue glow when disturbed by the surf near the shore. Scientists believe that bioluminescence evolved as a survival mechanism to distract predators, putting them off their game, so to speak, and also to alert and attract yet other predators that feed on the predators of the phytoplankton—further support for the basic premise that the enemy of my enemy is my friend. A pigment called luciferin and an enzyme called luciferase constitute the pair responsible for this light-producing reaction; a range of other creatures, including fireflies and jellyfish, employ the same duo to produce their own distinctive light shows. Doug Perrine, the photographer who took the striking photograph at right, was struck by another surprising phenomenon: "Every so often one of these bright specks of light would appear to take off and run up the beach." It turns out that ghost crabs were grabbing the glowing phytoplankton from the water and scurrying off to their burrows with them.

DOUG PERRINE/BARCROFT MEDIA/LANDOV

KAKADU MUDFLATS

The surrounding terrain might be bare, but the twisting rivers inside the Kakadu mudflats roll on

▶ This astonishing image was taken above the mudflats in northern Australia in Kakadu National Park, which, at 7,646 square miles, is the second largest national preserve in the world. Depending on the time of year, vistas like this one might be water filled or muddy, but the vegetation along the banks of the river thrives year round. Kakadu possesses an astonishing biodiversity, including 280 bird species, at least 60 mammal species, 50 freshwater fish species, 10,000 insect species and more than 1,600 plant species.

YANN ARTHUS-BERTRAND/CORBIS

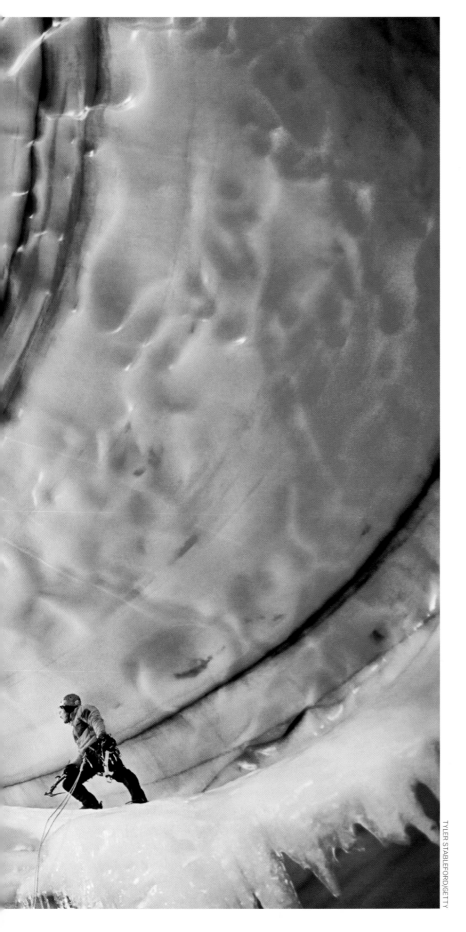

BLUE
ICE CAVE

Breathtaking vistas abound in the otherworldly caves beneath the massive glaciers in Iceland

▶ A photographer descended 80 feet below the surface of Langjokull Glacier in Iceland—the second largest glacier in Europe—to take this stunning image of one of the distinctive ice caves that form at the edge of glaciers in the region. The deeper one descends, the older the ice becomes, and the bluer it gets as the movement of the glacier compacts it further and further, driving out any air within the ice so that it absorbs any and all light, with the exception of a tiny amount in the blue spectrum, which is what is visible to the human eye, and to the eye of the camera. Such caves can be scary places, as even in the coldest months of winter, when the ice is uniformly rock hard, alarming cracking sounds can be heard every time the glacier moves even a millimeter. In Langjokull, a tunnel is being dug through the glacier to create a tourist destination, allowing visitors to descend comfortably 650 to 1,000 feet into the solid glacier ice, past breathtaking views of various caves and icy underground vistas. There will even be a chapel inside the cave to allow intrepid couples to tie the knot in this unusual and, for some, apparently romantic setting.

▶ The scale of the caves is truly mind-boggling, with some of the chambers measuring as high as 650 feet.

SON DOONG CAVE

In 2009, explorers discovered the world's largest cave in Vietnam

► In 1991, a local farmer in Quang Binh province in Vietnam stumbled on an enormous cave, created some two- to five-million years ago when a river eroded the limestone beneath the mountain near his village. The cave went unexplored in part because of the fearsome and strange whistling sounds that emanated from the cave's entrance, caused, it was later learned, by an underground river. But in 2009, the farmer led a joint British-Vietnamese expedition team to the site and what the team discovered instantly made headlines. Once they navigated the 262-foot drop into the cave, they found lush forests, an underground river more than a mile long, fields of algae, rare cave pearls the size of baseballs, and a massive stalagmite jutting from the cave floor that explorers named Hand of Dog. Flitting through the denser parts of the cave were monkeys and flying foxes. And when the team began trekking through the interior, they discovered just how vast the Son Doong Cave is—fully 5.5 miles long, with a chamber of the cave's interior measuring an astounding 650 feet high by 492 feet wide, dimensions that have established Son Doong as the largest cave in the world. The first tour groups began traveling into this enchanted underground space in 2013.

Please read about the GERENUK on page 81.

CURIOUS CREATURES

The fangs may look strange, but the tufted deer uses them to maximum effect when fighting its rivals.

1

CURIOUS CREATURES

The animal world offers an astonishing array of weird and wacky specimens. Here is a selection of our favorites.

1 **Tufted Deer** Not enough is known about this unusual looking member of the deer family. Relatively small—typically 20 to 28 inches high, 43 to 63 inches long and 37 to 110 pounds in weight—these deer are found almost exclusively in China and in forests at high altitude (up to 14,800 feet), making them difficult to study. Their name is derived from the tuft of hair typically sprouting from their heads, though the odd pair of canine teeth jutting out from the mouths of the males is considerably more eye-catching. These are largely solitary creatures and the male of the species, like some solemn security guard on a fixed route, will patrol its territory zealously and with regularity, using those nasty vampire-like teeth to repel any male competing for territory or for the attention of any potential mate. When faced with a predator, the tufted deer displays yet more eccentricity: After singing forth with a loud and startling bark, the animal will begin bounding away in a seemingly random zigzag pattern, its tiny white rump bouncing crazily around the terrain, thereby confusing its pursuers. Before the predator can regain its equilibrium, the tufted deer will flop to the ground to hide itself and, one would think, to catch its breath. While not yet officially endangered, the rapid rate of Chinese industrialization undoubtedly represents a threat to these unusual creatures.

2 **Gerenuk** The word *gerenuk* means "giraffe-necked" in the Somali language, and one look at this big-eared, small-mouthed antelope with its prominent neck makes it easy to see why it was so named. Found mostly in northeastern Africa, in semi-arid bushy terrain below 4,000 feet,

PREAU LOUIS-MARIE/HEMIS.FR/GETTY

▲ The gerenuk uses its long neck and legs to reach food others can't.

the gerenuk tends to avoid dangerously open grassy areas frequented by predators (lions, cheetahs, jackals and leopards) who lie in wait and remain near woody cover where, by standing on its hind legs and stretching its long neck, it can reach up to seven feet or so to pick at bushes and tree foliage generally only reachable by giraffes. When predators do appear, the gerenuk's exceptionally long legs enable it to flee at speeds of 35 to 40 miles per hour for up to four miles while bounding gracefully over obstacles of all sorts. Unfortunately those same long legs make the gerenuk prone to broken bones when one of those obstacles unexpectedly causes a trip or stumble. The gerenuk has one most unusual characteristic: As far as researchers can tell, the creature requires no water, getting all the moisture it needs from its diet, a trait that stands the gerenuk in exceptionally good stead in its often water-starved climate. Finally, it should be noted that the gerenuk is known as a "humble" beast by the Africans who are familiar with the species, prone to acts of heroism in assisting its friends in need.

3 **Saiga Antelope** For generations now, parents have been reading Dr. Seuss's fanciful tales to their children, marveling at the strange and exotic creatures that emerged from his fevered imagination. The notion that such creatures could exist in reality seemed extremely far-fetched, but in the wilds of Kazakhstan there is a type of antelope called a saiga, with a cartoonishly wide, bulbous proboscis, that for all the world looks like it emerged from the pages of a Seuss book. The saiga, an ancient antelope the size of a sheep that once shared the planet with the woolly mammoth during the Ice Age, has been teetering on the brink of extinction for decades, ever since the breakup of the Soviet Union led to unrestricted poaching driven by demand for the saiga horns used in traditional Chinese medicine as well as for saiga meat to feed the increasing numbers of rural poor. Thankfully, in recent years, conservation efforts have increased the size of the saiga herd in Kazakhstan, which had dipped to between 20,000 and 30,000, to more than 150,000 at last count. In some ways, the saiga would seem to be a relatively easy species to revive. Females begin giving birth at one year old, often have twins and triplets, and may produce as many as 20 calves in a lifetime. Furthermore, saigas typically give birth in massive groups over the course of a single week, offering more than typical protection to the calves, which are born with herds of adults surrounding them. On the other side of the ledger, though, is the plight of the males, who engage in a fight to the death—an astonishing 50 to 70 percent die in these battles—in order to establish themselves with a coterie of some dozen does. (During the height of the poaching period, the male population became so diminished—only males have the horns desired by poachers—that the ratio

KENNETH W. FINK/PHOTO RESEARCHERS/GETTY

3

▲The saiga antelope's proboscis serves several useful purposes.

of females to males became as high as 100 to 1.) Now the population is coming back and the steppes of Kazakhstan are again alive with the sometimes thundering herds that typify the massive migrations of these distinctive creatures. One final note: that Seussian proboscis is actually a miraculous instrument. During the summer months it filters out dust and in the winter it preheats the air before sending it down to the saiga's lungs.

4 **Pink Fairy Armadillo** The smallest armadillo species in the world, the pink fairy armadillo, at just 3.5 to 4.5 inches in length and a quarter of a pound in weight, can sit in the palm of a human hand. Like its larger armadillo cousins, the pink fairy armadillo has a shell on its top side, though its pinkish hue, derived from the animal's blood vessels which are visible through the shell, is unique to this tiny species. So is the extremely fine white hair visible from beneath the shell. Those blood vessels and that silky hair are both part of the creature's thermoregulation system that enables it to cope with the extreme variation in temperature in its habitat in central Argentina. Exposing more blood to chilly air or soil—making the carapace appear more pink—would lower the armadillo's body temperature, while draining the blood would enable the creature to hang on to the heat it needs during the colder periods at night, as would the hair, which acts as a kind of insulation. Unfortunately, these tiny marvels are extremely hard to study because they spend the bulk of their lives burrowing underground in search of ants and larvae, using their powerful claws on both their front and hind legs, which enable them to travel through the soil below ground at surprising rates of speed. The pink fairy armadillo is extremely sensitive to stress and none has survived in captivity for more than eight days or so. While habitat change, increasing use of pesticides and even a growing population of domestic cats and dogs are believed to be driving the pink fairy armadillo to near extinction, scientists have not been able to definitely determine the status of this elusive species.

▼The pink fairy armadillo is rarely seen above ground during the day.

NICHOLAS SMYTHE/PHOTO RESEARCHERS/GETTY

5 Okapi So God is feeling playful one night and says to himself, "I wonder what would happen if I took a giraffe, shrunk its neck just a bit, gave it a head that looks a little like a donkey with big ears, shaped its body to look like a horse, then added some zebra stripes to add a little pizzazz?" The result might be the okapi, a large (5 to 7 feet high at the shoulder, 6 to 8 feet long, 440 to 770 pounds) conglomerate creature which, if not the result of an evening of divine fun, might just have emerged from the drafting table of a mad scientist. In fact, this strange animal, most directly related to the giraffe, was unknown to the Western world until the early 20th century, when the first okapi was delivered to the Antwerp Zoo in 1918. (Previously, an animal that may have been an okapi was described in press reports about Congo explorer Sir Henry Morton Stanley in 1887, and Sir Harry Johnston, the British governor in Uganda, received a skull and bits of striped skin from native Pygmies that seemed definitive proof of the creature in 1901.) The lack of information about the okapi is not surprising—okapis tend to be secretive and solitary and they have always been hard to spot in the high mountain rainforests of central Africa where they traditionally lived. Today, the okapi, which, like its cousin the giraffe, uses its exceptionally long tongue—it can wash its eyelids and clean its ears with it— to snag leaves and buds from low-hanging tree branches, is rarely seen in the wild as its numbers in the Congo have dwindled to only approximately 10,000. The species is now officially recognized as endangered.

6 Fan-Throated Lizard Yes, there are lizards all over the world. And yes, they tend to look alike and to perform many of the same valuable functions for the ecological balance of the globe, most notably feeding on insects such as termites, beetles and grasshoppers, which might otherwise become more than a bit troublesome for the rest of us. So what is unusual about the fan-throated lizard? A quick look at the image below presents the most obvious answer. These eight-inch show-offs have a dewlap, or expandable fan of flesh under their throats, that can be puffed at will to display a rainbow of blue, black and red to attract females when the time is right, or alternatively to warn off predators or alert fellow lizards to a threat to the community. These colorful flaps are only possessed by the males, and not even by all of them; scientists do not seem to be clear as to why this is. The other odd characteristic of this particular lizard is that when it really wants to get motoring, it is able to stand up and run, quite quickly, on its two hind legs alone, presenting a comical sight to those lucky enough to witness it. To do so, you would have to travel to India, Sri Lanka or Pakistan.

◀ Is there a more unusual concatenation of features than in the endangered okapi?

▶ The colorful dewlap of the fan-throated lizard attracts females as well as warding off predators, apparently startled by this vivid flash of red.

THOMAS MARENT/MINDEN

CURIOUS CREATURES

JOEL SARTORE/NATIONAL GEOGRAPHIC/GETTY

7

▲They may not be pretty, but naked mole rats are part of an amazingly efficient society.

7 Naked Mole Rat It is a little surprising that when the Ugly Animal Preservation Society was holding its contest to name the world's ugliest creature (see page 17), the naked mole rat was not included on its list of candidates. Perhaps this is because, once you get past the naked mole rat's ungainly features, you discover that this is one of the world's most fascinating species. The lack of hair is indeed a bit creepy looking, but this allows the animals to stay relatively cool in the hot, arid desert environment of East Africa where they typically reside; at night, when temperatures drop, they huddle together in a massive pig pile to share the warmth of their bodies. Not fascinating enough? How about this? Those two massive front teeth you see above can be moved independently of one another to allow for maximum efficiency when the mole rat is attempting to deal with the oftentimes tough root or tuber-type vegetation it feeds on in its underground burrow. More interesting still, the naked mole rat is one of the only rodent species that is eusocial, meaning it operates within a highly organized social structure far more akin to that of an insect than of anything in the mammalian world. Its underground burrows can be up to

600 yards long, with a system of tunnels connecting the various chambers, each of which has a specific function, including a space for babies, a space where food is stored, a space for going to the bathroom and, of course, a place where the queen, the leader of a colony of up to 300 mole rats, resides in royal splendor. Queen is not a hereditary position—it is earned through fierce battle, after which the victor is able to actually stretch the distance between her vertebrae to become longer than her subjects, thereby further reinforcing her position as the leader of the clan. The queen is serviced by only a few select males; she may give birth to up to 27 babies at a time, four or five times a year. The rest of the males function as either food-gatherers—mole rats share their food without hesitation—or as soldiers of sorts, protecting the colony from any intruders. When faced with a snake in one of their tunnels, mole rats will form themselves into a ball of bodies blocking the tunnel and confronting the snake with a wall of fearsome teeth. One final oddity: mole rats appear to be surprisingly resistant to cancers, one reason why they are among the longest-living rodents in the world, sometimes reaching the age of 31. So yes, these creatures are not likely to win any beauty contests—they didn't win the ugly contest either—but they may be one of the smartest, most adaptable animals you'll ever meet.

8 Climbing Goats Goats are legendary for their climbing acumen, often negotiating extremely steep, mountainous terrain as they make their way about their sometime alpine habitats. But have you ever seen a goat climb a tree? As shown opposite, that is precisely what the goats of Morocco do in an effort to get their mouths on the delectable berries of the area's argan trees. As in the case of their mountain-climbing brethren, these goats display an almost uncanny sense of balance and sure-footedness (sure-hoofedness?) in climbing up the trunk and then balancing on the seemingly fragile branches in order to pluck the berries from the tree. A strange sidebar to this story: The goats will later excrete large kernels of the seeds from these berries, which will in turn be harvested, washed and pressed in order to generate the highly prized argan oil, mainly used for culinary and cosmetic purposes.

▶ Hunger and the love of argan berries motivated these resourceful goats to learn to climb trees.

▲The revival of the walking sticks began with the discovery of a hardy few remaining on Ball's Pyramid (above).

9 Lord Howe Island Walking Sticks Sometimes the sheer tenacity of the natural world is as wondrous as any unusual physical configuration, though the very large (up to six inches) Lord Howe Island walking stick—so named because it resembles a stick in motion—is most assuredly not your typical insect. (At one point it was also known as a tree lobster because of its size and its hard exoskeleton.) But this is more than a story of the world's heaviest flightless insect: More compellingly, this is a tale of a hardy survivor. Originally these creatures existed in some abundance only on Lord Howe Island, a smallish piece of property in the South Pacific. In 1918 a ship from Britain named the SS *Makambo* ran aground near the island. Along with the human evacuees were a number of black rats, which happily clambered onto Lord Howe Island and promptly began devouring the large, tasty insects. Soon the rats had multiplied and the walking sticks had been entirely eliminated.

This seemed to be the end of the line for the walking sticks, which had been on earth for millennia but now appeared destined for the dustheap of extinction. But in the 1960s, a team of climbers exploring Ball's Pyramid, a narrow finger of rock, 1,844 feet high, jutting out of the Pacific some 13 miles away from Lord Howe Island, claimed to have seen some walking-stick corpses on the steep slopes of the rock. This assertion went unexplored until 2001, when two Australian scientists and their assistants decided to make a trip to Ball's Pyramid to see what they could discover. To their surprise, they found 24 Lord Howe walking sticks living under and feeding off a single melaleuca bush some 330 feet up the face of the rock. Eventually, four insects were removed from the rock, and although two of them died, the other pair (appropriately known as Adam and Eve) established a new population of walking sticks at the Melbourne Zoo. The insects are unusual in their mating habits, with a

TUI DE ROY/MINDEN

▲ The olinguito is surprisingly adept at jumping from branch to branch in its arboreal environment.

single male and female pairing off for life. The mystery at the heart of this story, of course, remains unsolved: Just how did the walking sticks travel 13 miles across the sea from Lord Howe Island to Ball's Pyramid? Did they hop a ride with a local fisherman perhaps? Were they transported by bird? We will probably never know the answer, but, mystery or not, this tale of tenacity has a decidedly happy ending.

10 Olinguito When you live in the so-called cloud forests between 5,000 and 9,000 feet up in the Andes of western Colombia and Ecuador, it's easy to get missed. Throw in the fact that you tend to be nocturnal, solitary and even a tad reclusive, and the likelihood of being ignored grows even greater. Such was the fate of the olinguito, the first new species of carnivorous mammal to be identified in the Western Hemisphere in 35 years. You will note we use the term *identified* as opposed to *seen*, since we now know of at least one olinguito that was in several zoos but had been mistakenly identified as being a member of the larger, longer olingo family. Zoo staff had been baffled as to why the creature showed no interest in mating with the olingos until DNA finally proved that it was in fact a member of an entirely different species, a discovery that led researchers to the Andes to find examples of the new species in the wild. Having done so, the world was then alerted in 2013 to the existence of a new species, dubbed the olinguito, or "small olingo." Furrier than the olingo, with a shorter tail and smaller ears, the olinguito, which resembles a cross between a domestic cat and a teddy bear, is the smallest of the raccoon family at just two pounds and 13 to 17 inches long. And while the olinguito is technically a carnivore, it generally prefers fruit from its strictly arboreal environment—it jumps from tree to tree with great skill—along with a few insects and a touch of nectar every once in a while.

Please read about SULTAN KOSEN on page 95.

THE HUMAN FAMILY

ISLAND OF THE DOLLS

One man's inexplicable obsession led to this strange island of broken, deteriorating figurines that festoon the landscape

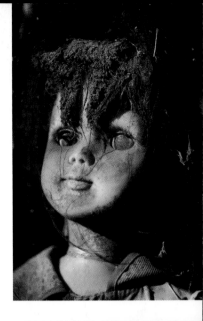

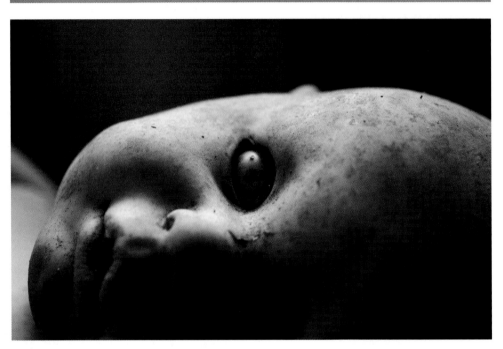

▶ While never officially diagnosed, it seems fair to say that Don Julian Santana Barrera was not of sound mind. Sometime in the early 1950s, Don Julian became obsessed with the death of a young girl in the canals near Xochimilco, just south of Mexico City, but the facts surrounding this event remain somewhat in dispute to this day. One legend suggests that Don Julian actually tried to save the girl but was unable to do so; others claim that the girl never even existed and that the supposed tragedy was simply a product of Don Julian's fevered imagination. The rest of the story is less uncertain: Don Julian left his wife and child, moved to a nearby island among the canals and began salvaging dolls he found in the water and in local rubbish bins and placing hundreds of them wherever he could and in whatever condition he found them all over the island. Some say he believed the dolls were possessed by the spirits of lost girls, but, regardless of his motivation, the result is one of the world's most bizarre landscapes, with dolls in various states of decay, some missing limbs or eyes or portions of their faces, festooning every available nook and cranny, including a fair number in Don Julian's own shack, where he dressed his personal dolls in a variety of garb. In a final note of irony, Don Julian himself drowned in 2001, some 50 years after he began collecting his dolls, allegedly in the same spot where the little girl who had inspired his obsession had perished so long ago. The island, little known during Don Julian's lifetime, has since become a major tourist attraction.

◀ Don Julian began by collecting the dolls that drifted past his home among the canals, but soon extended his search to include local rubbish bins as well.

▶ Dangi, who suffers from primordial dwarfism, is the world's shortest man, at 21.5 inches, barely more than one-fifth the size of his fellow record holder at the other end of the spectrum.

◀ Kosen, who officially stopped growing at last in 2012, holds the Guinness record for tallest man as well as for longest hands, measured at 11.22 inches from wrist to the tip of his middle finger.

THE LONG AND SHORT OF IT

One is from Turkey, the other from Nepal, but both reside at the extremes of the human family

▶ Human beings are indeed a diverse lot. And although there is nothing particularly useful about plumbing the degree of this self-evident variation, we are nonetheless fascinated by the extremes. No one knows this better than the folks who maintain the Guinness World Records, the repository of all things wild and wacky about the human condition. In just the past four years, Guinness has posted new records for two of the most closely watched marks: tallest and shortest man. The winner on the skyscraper side of the ledger is a part-time farmer from Turkey named Sultan Kosen, who was measured in 2011 at an astounding eight foot three inches tall. Kosen is a victim of a malfunction called pituitary gigantism, in which a tumor or some other malady damages the pituitary gland, causing it to release growth hormone far beyond the normal human developmental curve. Kosen, who also holds the record for largest hands (11.22 inches from wrist to the tip of middle finger), only began slowing the growth in 2010, when he underwent so-called "gamma-knife" surgery on the tumor affecting his pituitary gland at the University of Virginia School of Medicine, where he also received medication to control the growth-hormone levels. In March 2012,

doctors confirmed that Kosen's treatment had indeed finally stopped his growth, though he continues to need the assistance of crutches or a cane when walking. In a happy bit of recent news, Kosen got married in October 2013.

The short end of the record stick belongs to Chandra Bahadur Dangi from Reemkholi, an isolated village in Nepal, who was officially measured at 21.5 inches tall, knocking former champion Gul Mohammed (22 inches) off his very low pedestal. Dangi suffers from primordial dwarfism, one of the rarest of the 200 types of dwarfism, in which the individual is tiny by normal standards from the very beginning, even as a fetus. Dangi's village has only 200 homes, including a few solar panels for electricity and no televisions whatsoever. Dangi earns some money for his family—he lives with his brother—by fashioning placemats and head straps that allow his neighbors to help carry the heavy loads they often tote around on their backs.

Though representing startlingly divergent extremes, both men struggle with their condition but attest nonetheless to the resilience of the human spirit. In that way, they are far more alike than one might think.

THE FORGOTTEN HEIRESS

For the final 23 years of her life, Huguette Clark lived anonymously in hospitals while her mansions sat empty

► She was the daughter of one of the nation's richest men, a senator from Montana, copper magnate, railroad tycoon and one of the men responsible for the creation of a city in the desert that would come to be known as Las Vegas. She grew up surrounded by all the hallmarks of privilege: trips to Europe on luxurious cruise ships, hiking in the Grand Canyon, attendance at Manhattan's prestigious Spence School, fine art adorning the walls of the many homes she inhabited. There was a short-lived marriage in 1928 and a romantic attachment to her longtime painting instructor after that. But for reasons that remain mysterious to this day, the charmed life of Huguette Clark began unraveling as she moved into middle age. Might the death of her beloved older sister when Huguette was just a girl have been the beginning of her slide? And what of her breakdown in 1942, triggered apparently by her anxiety about World War II? Was she perhaps just constitutionally fragile, unable to deal with the world of hard knocks from which even her massive wealth could not protect her? Whatever the reason, as the years wore on, Huguette retreated further and further into her cosseted cocoon, seeing almost no one, distrusting her own family, becoming more and more isolated. She continued to support her many charities, particularly those associated with fine art—she was a longtime supporter of the Corcoran Gallery of Art in Washington, D.C.—but fewer and fewer people could say that they had actually seen her in person. Finally, when she was taken to the hospital in 1988 with cancerous lesions on her face, she simply decided to stay, eventually settling in Beth Israel Medical Center, where she lived, anonymously, for the next 23 years until her death in 2011 at the age of 104. During those years of her hospitalization, while she was cared for by private nurses, seeing few others besides her attorney, her accountant, and a dear friend or two, her many properties, including an estate in Santa Barbara, a large home in New Canaan, Connecticut, and her three large apartments in Manhattan, all sat empty, carefully maintained by staff, but

▲ When Huguette (above) was just four years old, she moved with her family into a 121-room mansion at Fifth Avenue and 77th Street in Manhattan (opposite).

unoccupied, gilded cages without the captive who once lived there. Her will was the subject of controversy and litigation, with her family, many of whom had not seen her in decades, objecting to several of the bequests, including a particularly large one to a longtime nurse, but in the end the courts upheld her decision to leave the bulk of her $300 million fortune to charity.

MISS JULIA PASTRANA;
THE EMBALMED NONDESCRIPT EXHIBITING AT 191 PICCADILLY. Jany 1862.

▲ After years in an Oslo research institute, Pastrana's body was finally buried properly in 2013.

INNOCENCE EXPLOITED

Julia Pastrana was a tragic victim of her era's cruel intolerance

▶ Human cruelty has taken many forms through the centuries, but the tale of Julia Pastrana surely represents one of the more sordid chapters in that long history. Born in Mexico in 1834, Pastrana had two ailments: hypertrichosis lanuginosa, which resulted in thick hair sprouting all over her body, and gingival hyperplasia, which caused her lips and gums to thicken to nearly simian proportions. In an era when traveling "freak shows" that gleefully exhibited all manner of human deformation were touring the world, Pastrana's particular constellation of features clearly meant money for those unscrupulous enough to exploit her condition. The most notable of these was a man named Theodore Lent, who first became her manager and then her husband, billing her in his shows as "the ugliest woman in the world," or as a "bear-woman" or an "ape-woman." The popular press was happy to pile on, with the esteemed *New York Times* running an ad that called her the "link between mankind and the ourang-outang" and European

newspapers calling her "revolting in the extreme." When she died five days after giving birth in 1860, at the age of only 26, rather than giving his wife a proper burial, Lent chose to have her embalmed along with their son who also died soon after birth and who inherited his mother's hypertrichosis, so he could continue to tour with their remains. He even found a bearded woman in Germany whom he paid to tour as Pastrana's sister.

There are few grace notes in this sad tale, though an 1868 book by natural historian Francis Buckland humanized Pastrana to some extent by describing her sweet singing voice, her linguistic proficiency and her charitable giving. And, in 2013, through the concerted effort of New York–based visual artist Laura Anderson Barbata, Pastrana's body was finally retrieved from an Oslo research institute and returned to her homeland of Sinaloa, Mexico, where she received what even the most scorned among us surely deserve: a proper burial.

WINCHESTER MYSTERY HOUSE

Until Sarah Winchester died in 1922, she never stopped building and rebuilding her eccentric California home

most unusual structures in the world. Stairways lead nowhere, doors open on to walls, entire sections of the house are closed off and passageways seem to go in circles, many of them with secret panels that send the traveler off in odd and unexpected directions. There is real beauty here as Winchester spared no expense—all the floors are parquet, with mahogany, rosewood, teak, maple, oak and white ash arranged in lovely mosaic patterns; the house is filled with Tiffany windows, silver and bronze inlaid doors, molded bathtubs

▶ A somewhat batty woman with far too much money and time on her hands can produce some pretty crazy stuff. That seems to be the lesson of the bizarre Winchester house in San Jose, California, built—though never really finished—over 38 years by Sarah Winchester, the widow of William Winchester, heir to a fortune generated by the Winchester Repeating Arms Company, the outfit that developed the repeating rifle so widely used in the inexorable American expansion into the West that followed the Civil War. Sarah's daughter died soon after birth in 1866 and when her husband died of tuberculosis 15 years later, the 43-year-old Winchester decided to consult a medium in hopes of understanding the reason for these tragedies. The medium informed her that the Winchester family had been cursed as a result of the many deaths produced by its rifles and that the only way to appease the spirits that were haunting the family was to build them a house and to keep building the house continuously, 365 days a year, ad infinitum. The result of all this activity is surely one of the

and elaborately crafted cabinetry. (One worker focused exclusively on the floors for 33 years.) The story is that Winchester would hold a séance every night to get direction from the spirits; she would then pass along the results to her long-suffering but probably very well paid foreman in the morning. Rooms would be started and then torn down or boarded up, a paint color would be applied, only to be repainted the next day, a great event like the 1906 earthquake might come along and persuade Winchester that the spirits wanted an entire section of the house closed. It is said that there are 160 rooms in the house, which is now a tourist destination, but no one is really certain as it is almost impossible to navigate the entire structure without getting lost. Winchester herself allegedly slept in a different bedroom every night—apparently she felt that such constant movement could protect her from the more malevolent spirits. In the end, however, she died in 1922 in her favorite bedroom, her debt fully paid, one hopes, to the spirits that surrounded her.

▶ Stairways leading nowhere, windows that open on walls, passageways with secret panels unknown to visitors—these are just a few of the odd features of the Winchester Mystery House.

THE HUMAN MYSTERY

The more we learn, the less we know: That is one clear lesson from the latest finds regarding the origins of our enigmatic species

▶ Science never proceeds in a straight line. Two steps forward, one step back; one dead end abandoned, another promising lead followed. That has been the nature of scientific discovery ever since the first humans began using their brains to explore their world. Of course who those first humans actually were and where they came from is as subject to the meandering methodology of science as any other area of inquiry, perhaps even more so in fact. Two important discoveries since 2008 simply serve to reinforce just how much remains to be learned about the origin of our own species. First there was the discovery of fossils in South Africa that pointed to a new human species, named *Australopithecus sediba*, endowed with characteristics of the *Homo* species as well as of other Australopithecene species, notably *Australopithecus africanus*. Similar to *Homo* species, *sediba* walked upright, had human-like hips and pelvises, small teeth and a more modern face than some of the species of *Australopithecus*. On the other hand, *sediba* had long ape-like arms for climbing through trees, but primitive feet and a tiny brain. Was this newly discovered species, which lived nearly two million years ago, the sought-after link between *Australopithecus* and *Homo*? Most experts have seen *Australopithecus africanus* as the most likely link. Might *africanus* have led to *sediba*, which in turn led to *Homo habilis*, which in turn led to *Homo erectus*, and then, eventually, much later, to *Homo sapiens*? Or might *sediba* have led to another species of *Homo* that ultimately disappeared? Might it have developed independently from *africanus*?

Mystery surrounds the various hominins that came along much later as well. In 2013, scientists were able

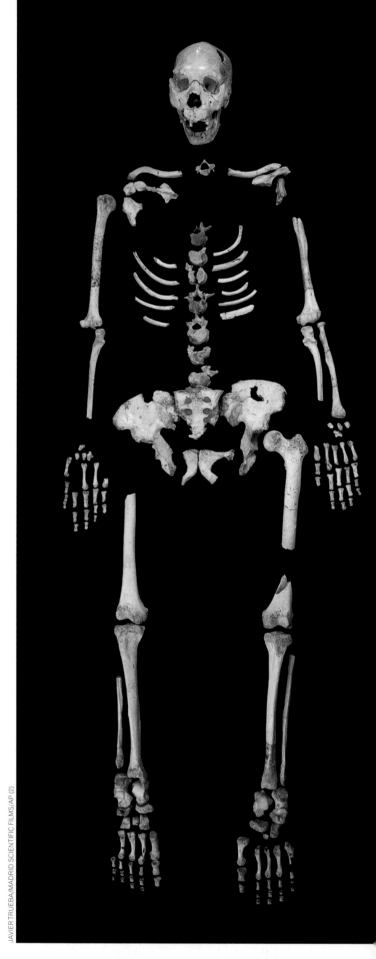

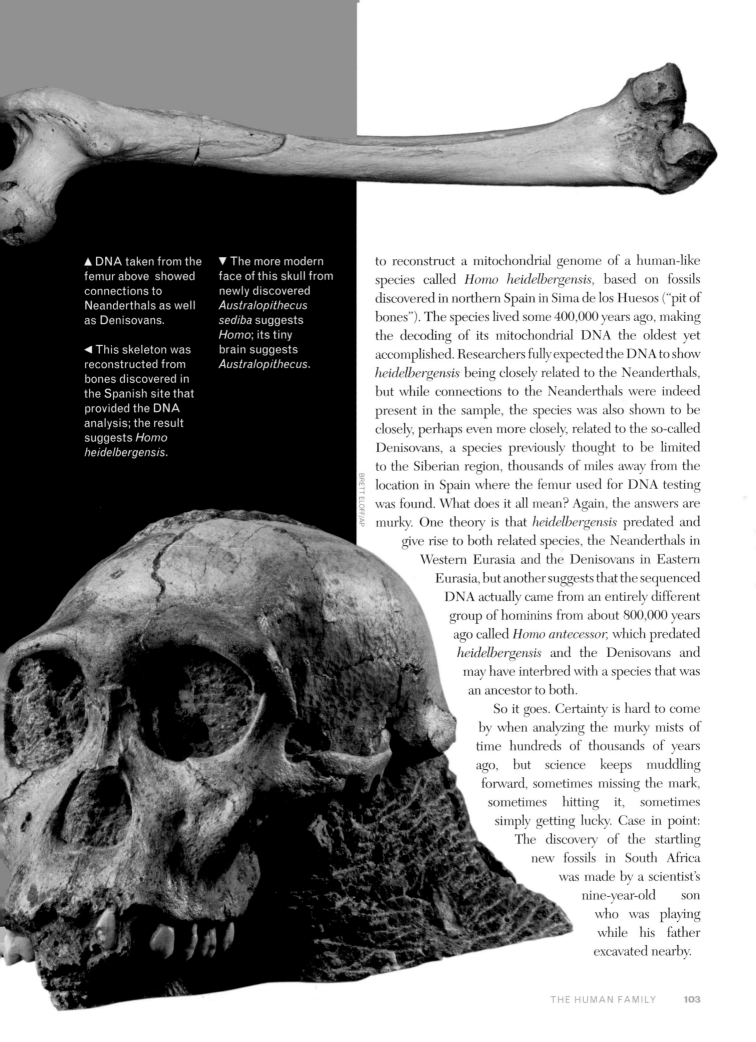

▲ DNA taken from the femur above showed connections to Neanderthals as well as Denisovans.

◄ This skeleton was reconstructed from bones discovered in the Spanish site that provided the DNA analysis; the result suggests *Homo heidelbergensis.*

▼ The more modern face of this skull from newly discovered *Australopithecus sediba* suggests *Homo*; its tiny brain suggests *Australopithecus.*

BRETT ELOFF/AP

to reconstruct a mitochondrial genome of a human-like species called *Homo heidelbergensis,* based on fossils discovered in northern Spain in Sima de los Huesos ("pit of bones"). The species lived some 400,000 years ago, making the decoding of its mitochondrial DNA the oldest yet accomplished. Researchers fully expected the DNA to show *heidelbergensis* being closely related to the Neanderthals, but while connections to the Neanderthals were indeed present in the sample, the species was also shown to be closely, perhaps even more closely, related to the so-called Denisovans, a species previously thought to be limited to the Siberian region, thousands of miles away from the location in Spain where the femur used for DNA testing was found. What does it all mean? Again, the answers are murky. One theory is that *heidelbergensis* predated and give rise to both related species, the Neanderthals in Western Eurasia and the Denisovans in Eastern Eurasia, but another suggests that the sequenced DNA actually came from an entirely different group of hominins from about 800,000 years ago called *Homo antecessor,* which predated *heidelbergensis* and the Denisovans and may have interbred with a species that was an ancestor to both.

So it goes. Certainty is hard to come by when analyzing the murky mists of time hundreds of thousands of years ago, but science keeps muddling forward, sometimes missing the mark, sometimes hitting it, sometimes simply getting lucky. Case in point: The discovery of the startling new fossils in South Africa was made by a scientist's nine-year-old son who was playing while his father excavated nearby.

Please read about the MARQUES DE RISCAL hotel on page 109.

MARVELS OF
THE MIND

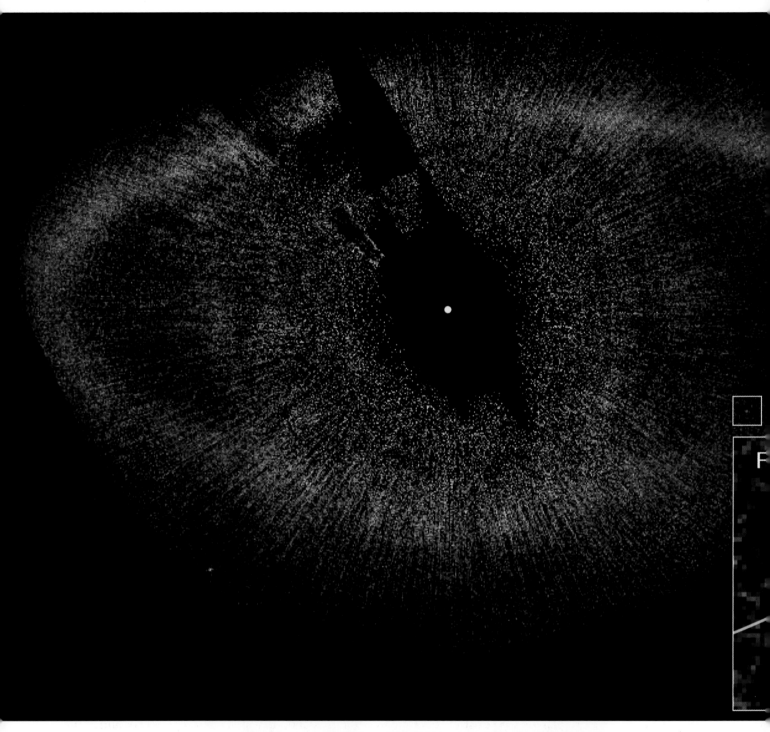

KEPLER SPACE TELESCOPE

This innovative high-tech device is sending back massive quantities of information about the world beyond our solar system

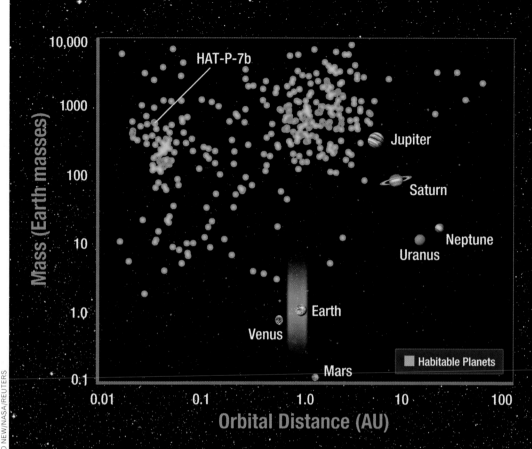

HO NEW/NASA/REUTERS

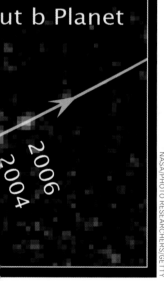

NASA/PHOTO RESEARCHERS/GETTY

▲ One exoplanet is called Fomalhaut b, named for the star around which it orbits at a distance of some 10.7 billion miles; the telesope identified Hat-P-7b (above, right), a planet the size of Jupiter 1,000 light years from Earth, in 2009.

▶ As the unstoppable engine of human ingenuity has been applied to astronomy, our capacity to understand and map the world beyond our own solar system has increased exponentially. No piece of new technology has been more crucial to this effort than NASA's remarkable Kepler space telescope, which has been relaying information back to Earth since 2009. Among its more stunning recent discoveries has been the existence of another 715 so-called exoplanets, that is, planets that exist outside our own solar system, bringing the total number of such celestial bodies to approximately 1,700. The vast majority of the new planets are between the size of Earth and the size of Neptune, and all of them exist within multiplanet systems—305 of them to be precise—in generally tight orbits around their suns and more tightly bunched with the other planets in their solar system than the planets are in ours. The telescope detects these planets by looking for the characteristic dimming of stars resulting from a planet passing in front of its star in direct alignment with the observing telescope, an event so reliant on chance that scientists believe that the telescope is still only detecting a fraction of the likely exoplanets out there. Among the newly discovered planets there are four that exist in an environment known as a "habitable zone," in which the temperatures and other conditions are right for water, or oceans, to exist, making it possible that some form of life might exist there. On the other hand, all four planets are more than twice the width of Earth, which may mitigate against the possibility of life. A new Kepler mission (Kepler 2) went operational in June 2014, and scientists expect it to yield 100 additional new planets a year.

►The ribbons on Gehry's creation reflect the Marqués de Riscal wine bottle as well as the pink hue of its classic Rioja wine.

MARQUÉS
DE RISCAL

Frank Gehry brings both whimsy and functionality to a luxury hotel and wine complex in northern Spain

▶ Creativity meets functionality in a unique way when talking about architecture, and few have brought more fanciful form to function than iconic architect Frank Gehry. His most famous creation may be the stunning Guggenheim Museum in Bilbao in northern Spain, but have you seen his transformation, just 70 miles south, of the Marqués de Riscal winery? The result is a sort of wine complex, with a five-star hotel, spa, museum of viticulture and wine shop completing the stunning package. As usual in Gehry designs, the end product resembles a three-dimensional abstract expressionist painting, or in this case, an elegant multifaceted gift package, topped by a winding ribbon that gives the whole a festive, holiday feeling. The materials used are Gehry favorites, with that ribbon-like roof composed of steel and titanium, and the colors of the ribbon reflecting the winery product: pink for the famed Rioja wine, silver for the foil that shields the corks, and gold for the mesh that appears on every bottle produced by Marqués de Riscal. The interior of the hotel reflects the whimsy of the exterior, with sloped walls and slanted cathedral ceilings looming overhead as guests are coddled in luxurious comfort below. How was Gehry persuaded to design his first hotel? No one knows for sure, but the bottle he was given by the winery, vintage 1929, the year of Gehry's birth, surely didn't hurt.

► Forestiere was able to create underground environments open to enough sun to enable his beloved fruit trees to flourish.

THE CATACOMBS OF
BALDASSARE FORESTIERE

Unschooled in design, this Sicilian immigrant nonetheless created an underground masterpiece

▶ When 22-year-old Baldassare Forestiere fled the oppressive grip of his father in Sicily to begin a new life in America, his plan was to grow fruit on the property he had purchased in Fresno, California. But upon his arrival in his new home, he was stunned to discover that his land was too dry and too hard to support the farm he had imagined. For many, this bitter pill might have been enough to persuade them to give up, perhaps even to return to Sicily. But Forestiere was made of sterner stuff, and, rather than surrender to the unyielding land and the unbearably hot sun of the Fresno summers, he returned to an inspiration from his youth—the Roman catacombs—and began what would be an astonishing 40-year project to build beneath ground what the world above ground would not provide him. Using no blueprints and without any formal training in design, and with no technology to aid him but traditional farmer's tools (picks, shovels, wheelbarrows and a scraper pulled by his two beloved mules, Dolly and Molly), Forestiere constructed a magical underground world on three levels (10 feet deep, 22 feet deep and 23 feet deep) over 10 acres, complete with a parlor with fireplace, a summer and winter bedroom, a courtyard with fish pond and a fully equipped kitchen. Through the ingenious use of skylights and carefully crafted tunnels to the surface, he was able to get enough light into the subterranean spaces to grow vines and trees bearing a variety of fruit— oranges, tangerines, sweet and sour lemons, grapefruits, pomegranates, pears, persimmons, almonds, palm dates and strawberries—as well as to provide ways for the heat to escape, while the cool air remained below. While his contemporaries sweltered without air conditioning in the above-ground world, Forestiere luxuriated in his naturally cooled catacombs below. The stonework

▲ Simplicity and classic Italian elegance are both in ample evidence in Forestiere's unforgettable home.

throughout this underground oasis is astonishingly beautiful, with numerous grottos and arches and patios and gardens that echo the creator's Italian heritage and influences. Forestiere never married—one woman refused to marry him unless he built her a home above ground—but his family continues to burnish his legacy and his remarkable subterranean creation is now on the National Register of Historic Places.

THE TAYLOR SCULPTURES

These stunning underwater creations are aesthetically pleasing and environmentally essential

▶ There are those who view art as a frivolous pursuit, something that serves little purpose in our utilitarian world of hard-nosed commerce. We do not subscribe to this view in any case, but such a position seems particularly indefensible when faced with the elegant and eye-catching work of Jason deCaires Taylor, a British sculptor who has made it his life's work to create environmentally sustainable sculptures to be installed in the sea, eventually to become artificial coral reefs desperately needed in a seriously depleted underwater ecosystem. His human figures are all based on life casts of actual, living people, and the materials used—marine-grade cement, microsilica and sand, with the occasional inclusion of ceramic tiles and glass—combine to produce a statue of 95 percent inert materials, offering the perfect surfaces for the growth of coral. Taylor has installed his sculptures in a variety of locations, including Grenada, Kent and Chepstow in England, Greece and most recently Cancun, Mexico, where his collection of 403 life-size figures shown below and titled "The Silent Evolution" represents his largest installation to date, covering an area of more than 459 square yards, potentially a coral reef of significant dimensions.